THE
Desperate Act

Austria-Hungary and the Balkan states in 1914.

The Slavic provinces of the Austro-Hungarian empire.

THE
Desperate Act

The Assassination of
Franz Ferdinand at Sarajevo

by Roberta Strauss Feuerlicht

McGRAW-HILL BOOK COMPANY
New York • Toronto • London • Sydney

Library of Congress Catalog Number: 68-17505

1234567890 VBVB 7543210698

Author's Note

There is a story in every book and there is a story behind every book—the story of why it was written. In the spring of 1963, while gathering material for a book on Yugoslavia, I came in time to the assassination of Franz Ferdinand at Sarajevo. When I checked the birth and death dates of each of the assassins, I was startled by the fact that two of them were still alive. This seemed impossible until I realized that in 1914 they were only in their teens.

I went to Yugoslavia that summer and met one of the surviving assassins, Dr. Cvetko Popović; the other one refuses to see foreign journalists. There were two long and cordial interviews with Dr. Popović in July and September, and what he said so intrigued me that I put aside the book on Yugoslavia—which is still unwritten—and began work on this book instead. In addition, I wrote an article based on my interviews with Dr. Popović. The article appeared in the *Saturday Evening Post* on the fiftieth anniversary of the assassination.

I returned to Yugoslavia in the summer of 1967 to

complete my research and again met with Dr. Popović. Now in his seventies, he admits that his recollection of what happened in 1914 is dimming. In spite of this, or perhaps because of it, he feels strongly that almost everything ever written on the subject of the assassination is somehow wrong, including my article. I found him at work on a book that would correct everyone else's errors, after which he planned to publish his own account.

As he grows older, Dr. Popović appears to want to recast the events in a more heroic mold. To do this, he has begun to deny his own words, both from his interviews with me and from a series of articles he wrote in 1928. Earlier, he could still see the story whole, faintly absurd as well as highly tragic. Now, however, he objects to any phrase or fact, whether trivial or important, if in his view it diminishes the role of any of the assassins.

Nonetheless, Dr. Popović remains one of the best sources for material about the assassination. He is particularly valuable when he describes the motives and feelings of the assassins, especially his own. I have therefore used many quotes both from his articles and from my interviews with him. Although the quotes are accurate and in context, Dr. Popović is in no other way responsible for the contents of this book.

Dr. Popović's articles were originally published in the Yugoslav newspaper *Politika,* and I wish to thank *Politika* for giving me permission to excerpt this mater-

ial. The translation is by Professor Aleksandar Ar-
anicki. I would also like to thank Vasiljka Prelević,
the curator of the Mlada Bosna and Gavrilo Princip
Museum, for making available to me all but one of
the historical photographs used in this book. The
photographs of Sarajevo today were taken by my husband, Herbert A. Feuerlicht, who also drew the map
of Franz Ferdinand's route, and to whom I am grateful for the countless ways he assisted me in the long
trek across Princip's Bridge.

Roberta Strauss Feuerlicht
Sarajevo, Yugoslavia
June 28, 1967

CONTENTS

PRONUNCIATION AND TERMS

The words *Serb* and *Serbian* are sometimes used interchangeably, but not in this book. Here they have two distinct meanings. *Serb* is used to describe the members of a particular ethnic group. *Serbian* is used to describe the inhabitants of Serbia, no matter what their origin. A Serb, therefore, does not have to be a Serbian, and a Serbian does not have to be a Serb. The words *Croat* and *Croatian* are used the same way.

Serbo-Croatian, the language of the Yugoslavs, is difficult for the average Westerner to pronounce, but English is just as difficult for the average Yugoslav. The consonants that are pronounced least like they look are:

c = ts	j = y
ć = tch	š = sh
č = ch	ž = zh

Sarajevo is pronounced "Sa-rai-ye-vo," with a slight accent on the first syllable.

MAJOR CHARACTERS

Gavrilo Princip
Nedeljko Čabrinović
Trifun Grabež
Mehmed Mehmedbašić   the assassins of Franz Ferdinand
Vaso Čubrilović
Cvetko Popović

Danilo Ilić
Veljko Čubrilović   the leading accomplices
Mihajlo Jovanović

11

Colonel Apis	leader of the Black Hand
Franz Josef	Emperor of Austria-Hungary
Franz Ferdinand	heir to the Austrian throne
Sophie Chotek	wife of Franz Ferdinand
General Oskar Potiorek	governor of Bosnia and Hercegovina
Miloš Obilić	assassin of Sultan Murad in 1389
Bogdan Žerajić	would-be assassin of Governor Varešanin in 1910

No government can have a right to obedience from a people who have not freely consented to it.

John Locke, *Of Civil Government*

Prologue

In the city of Sarajevo, the morning of June 28, 1914, dawned sunny and hot. Sarajevo was the capital of Bosnia, a distant province of the Austro-Hungarian empire. On that summer day, Archduke Franz Ferdinand, heir to the Austrian throne, was to honor the city with a royal visit.

Franz Ferdinand was scheduled to arrive in Sarajevo by train at about 9:30 A.M. After a brief review of the troops at an Austrian army camp opposite the railroad station, he would be driven in an open car to the town hall. His route led along the Appel Quay, a narrow, curving street built by the Austrians. One side of the quay is bordered by houses and shops. On the other side is a low embankment that overlooks the blood-red waters of the Miljačka River.

The citizens of Sarajevo prepared to receive Franz Ferdinand, each in his own way. Some decorated their homes with the black-and-yellow flag of Austria, placed portraits of the Archduke in their windows, and went down to the quay to wish him long life as he passed. Others, however, found no reason to cheer.

15

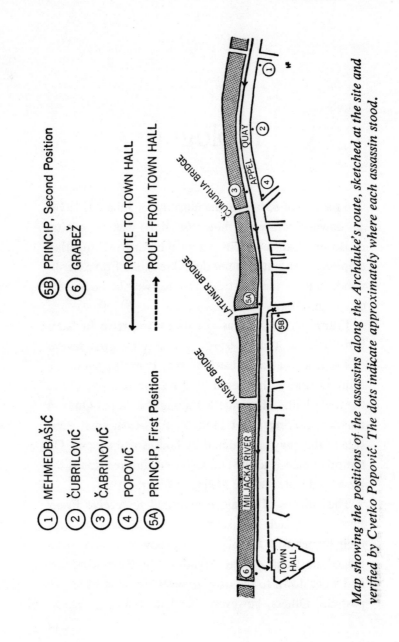

MEHMEDBAŠIĆ
ČUBRILOVIĆ
ČABRINOVIĆ
POPOVIĆ
PRINCIP, First Position
PRINCIP, Second Position
GRABEŽ

ROUTE TO TOWN HALL
ROUTE FROM TOWN HALL

MILJACKA RIVER
KAISER BRIDGE
LATEINER BRIDGE
ĆUMURIJA BRIDGE
APPEL QUAY
TOWN HALL

Map showing the positions of the assassins along the Archduke's route, sketched at the site and verified by Cvetko Popović. The dots indicate approximately where each assassin stood.

For them, Austria was a tyranny and Franz Ferdinand was a tyrant.

Early that morning, a short, slender, eighteen-year-old student named Cvetko Popović had greeted the sun with dismay, for he had counted on wearing his long black cape that day. It had been raining in Sarajevo for several days and, in the rain, a cape would not seem conspicuous. The local students often wore them because they cost less than overcoats. To wear a heavy wool cape on such a sunny day, however, might arouse suspicion. But if he didn't wear it, someone might see the strange bulges in the pockets of his jacket. He considered the alternatives and made his decision. Drawing the cape over his shoulders, he stepped out into the sunlight.

As he walked through the streets of Sarajevo, Popović unscrewed the cap of a small, flat, rectangular bomb and slipped the bomb into the right-hand pocket of his jacket. He cocked a pistol and stuffed it into his left-hand pocket. One of his pockets already held a twist of cigarette paper filled with poison.

When he reached the Appel Quay, Popović recognized another Bosnian student, nineteen-year-old Gavrilo Princip. Popović knew that Princip had not been in Sarajevo recently. Why had Princip returned? Popović wondered if they were at the river embankment for the same purpose.

After first stopping at his school, Popović walked to a prearranged position near the corner of Appel Quay

17

and Čumurija Street. There he halted in front of a to-bacco shop. Princip, meanwhile, had walked farther up the embankment. He stood near the Lateiner Bridge, on the river side of the street. Popović's guess was correct; Princip also carried a gun, a bomb, and poison.

Four others were waiting along the Appel Quay. The first was a twenty-seven-year-old carpenter, Meh-med Mehmedbašić. Next was a seventeen-year-old student, Vaso Čubrilović. Farther up the quay, diag-onally opposite Popović, was a nineteen-year-old type-setter, Nedeljko Čabrinović. Another student, eighteen-year-old Trifun Grabež, stood along the em-bankment about two blocks beyond Princip.

All six were armed—with guns or bombs or both. All had come to the Appel Quay that sunny summer morning to murder Franz Ferdinand.

1 · Enslavement

Political murder is not the work of a moment, nor is it the whim of a madman. The events of June 28, 1914, had roots that ran centuries deep. A direct line sprang from another June 28, which was also sunny and hot. The year was 1389 and the place was a vast plateau some 125 miles southeast of Sarajevo. It is called Kosovo Polje, or the Field of Blackbirds. There, as the sun broke through a night of rain, two mighty armies clashed for possession of the Balkan peninsula, the mountainous link between Europe and Asia.

Defending their land was an army composed mainly of Serbians and led by a Serbian prince named Lazar. The Serbs are a Slavic people, who probably settled in the Balkans during the seventh century. For hundreds of years they were subjects of the Byzantine empire. Then, in the twelfth and thirteenth centuries, a line of powerful rulers forged an independent Serbian state. The state soon became a kingdom and, in time, an empire. In 1345, in the gold and purples of royalty, the Serbian ruler, Dušan, was crowned emperor of the Serbs, the Greeks, the Bulgarians, and the Albanians. The Serbians were now masters of the Balkan peninsula.

But Dušan was not content. He envisioned a Serbian empire succeeding Byzantium as the major power in southeast Europe. With an army of 80,000 men, Dušan set out to conquer Constantinople, the capital of the Byzantine empire. But in December, 1355, on the outskirts of the city, Dušan died suddenly and painfully, probably of poison.

With Dušan died the dream of Serbian glory. His nineteen-year-old son was too weak to hold the Serbian empire together. Warring nobles tore Dušan's empire apart. At the same time that Dušan's empire was breaking up into small feudal states, the Turks began their march into Europe. Turkey was a military state with an almost invincible army. Wolves followed the path of the Turkish troops to feed upon the corpses. In 1371, the Turks conquered Macedonia, the southernmost province of what had been the Serbian empire. Now the heart of the Balkan peninsula lay open to them.

In 1389 the Turks confronted the Serbians at Kosovo Polje. Their sultan, Murad, led an immense army estimated at over 80,000 cavalry, infantry, and archers. "Their tents stretched like the snow in winter," according to one description.

The most important Serbian prince was Lazar. Knowing that the battle with Murad would determine the future of the Balkans, he prepared for it. He made alliances with other leaders, including King Tvrtko of Bosnia. Bosnia, a land that bordered Lazar's territory to the northwest, had also been settled by Serbs. Prince Lazar imported arms for the battle from as far away as Italy. Guns may have been used but no one is certain, for details of the encounter at Kosovo Polje are scant and much disputed. The clash produced poets rather than historians.

The battle began at daybreak on June 28, which is the feast day of St. Vitus, or Vidovdan, and ended in the afternoon. A report written at the time said, "There was great slaughter, as much among the Turks as the Serbians, and few returned to their own country. . . . Victory was not granted either to the Turks or the Serbians, so great was the carnage." A Turkish account described the battlefield as looking "like a tulip bed, with its ruddy severed heads and rolling turbans."

Although the Turks did not actually win at Kosovo, the battle became the central tragedy of Serbian history. For Prince Lazar was slain, and the Serbians were without a champion. Seeking life in death, Serbian minstrels later sang of their loss as though it had been a great victory. A gray falcon had flown to Lazar's castle on the eve of the battle, they said, and in its beak it bore a message from the Virgin Mary. She asked Lazar if he wanted an earthly kingdom or a heavenly one. If he wanted an earthly kingdom, he would defeat the Turks; if he wanted a heavenly kingdom, he would be defeated.

"An earthly kingdom is but fleeting, but God's kingdom shall endure forever," replied Lazar. He chose the heavenly kingdom, and his wish was granted. At some point during the battle he was captured by the Turks and beheaded.

The Turkish leader, Sultan Murad, also died at Kosovo, the victim of an assassin. As told in the Serbian ballads, Prince Lazar held a great banquet the night before the battle. When the time came for a toast, Lazar raised his golden goblet to one of his nobles, Miloš Obilić. "To none will I drink but thee," said the Prince. "Tomorrow on Kosovo thou wilt betray me."

Miloš leaped to his feet in anger. "Traitor I am not, was not, will never be," he replied. "Rather, on the field of Kosovo will I perish in defense of my faith. My hand shall slay the Turkish sultan, my foot shall stand upon his neck."

No one knows if Lazar really did accuse Miloš of treason. But on Vidovdan, Miloš Obilić went to the Sultan's camp. He said he had deserted Lazar and had come to fight with the glorious Murad. Flattered, the Sultan invited Miloš to kiss his foot. As the Serbian noble came forward, he drew a dagger from his sleeve and stabbed Murad. Miloš was slashed to pieces by the Sultan's guards, but the Turkish tyrant was dead.

Though the leaders of both armies died at Kosovo,

the loss was greater for the Serbians. Lazar's death left no one strong enough to unify the Balkan peoples. Effective resistance to the Turks collapsed, and during the fifteenth century, they took possession of the peninsula. By 1459 a Serbian state no longer existed. Bosnia fell in 1463. Hercegovina, a semi-independent state in the south of Bosnia, fell soon after.

The only Serbs who were never really conquered by the Turks were those who took refuge in the stark cliffs along the western coast of the peninsula, in the area called the Black Mountain, or Montenegro. The Montenegrins later adopted a national costume with a round, black-and-red pillbox cap. According to tradition, the red crown of the cap represents the blood shed at Kosovo, and the black border is in mourning for the defeat. Thus, for Serbs everywhere, Kosovo Polje was hallowed as the grave of their freedom, Vidovdan became a day of sorrow, and Miloš Obilić was hailed as a national hero, for he had given his life to slay the oppressor.

"For more than three centuries and a half the Southern Slavs disappear from the pages of history." This is the way one historian describes the period of Turkish occupation. A darkness fell over the Serb lands—the darkness of oppression. The Turks sent in their governors and their troops, and took out taxes in both money and blood. The blood tax was on eight-year-old boys who were taken from their native villages, brought up as Moslems, and trained to be soldiers in the sultan's army.

Although they were outwardly conquered, the Serbians never ceased to be rebels. Just as their dances and songs and poems were passed from father to son, so was the vow that Kosovo would be avenged. Even under Turkish rule the Serbians kept their customs and beliefs. Centuries earlier, the Catholic Church had divided. There was the Roman Catholic Church, ruled by Rome, and the Eastern Orthodox Church, ruled by Constantinople. The Serbians belonged to a branch of the Eastern Church. During the years of oppression the Serbian Orthodox Church helped nurture the people's spirit of identity as well as their spirit of rebellion.

The Serbians did not rest quietly in Turkish hands, and from the first there were revolts. But the Turks crushed them easily and went on to menace central Europe with conquest. The Turks beseiged Vienna, the capital of Austria, in 1529 and were turned back, but by the middle of the century they ruled most of Hungary. In the seventeenth century, however, a series of bad rulers weakened Turkey. A second Turkish assault on Vienna failed, and the invincible Turks began to retreat before the armies of Austria. In 1699 Turkey surrendered to Austria her Hungarian territory and two provinces, Croatia and Slavonia, which were inhabited by South Slavs. Turkey was no longer advancing in Europe; she was pulling back and leaving her possessions behind as she went. Austria had picked up three of the pieces, and her appetite was sharpened for more. She hoped to move down the Balkan peninsula until she won access to the Aegean Sea.

During the eighteenth century, Austria and Turkey fenced each other for control of the Balkans, which lay between them. Meanwhile, a third major power, Russia, decided that the Balkans were important to her own desire to control the Black Sea and gain access to the Mediterranean.

Though all the major powers in Europe developed strong convictions about the value of Balkan real estate, none of them seemed to care much about the suffering of the Balkan people. As the Turkish empire grew weaker, it became more oppressive. Taxes rose and cruelties were more common. Finally, in 1804, the Serbians rose in rebellion against the Turks. For a quarter of a century the Serbians combined bitter warfare with skillful negotiations in an attempt to win their freedom. They were supported by both Russia and Austria. Both powers were eager to increase their influence in the Balkans at Turkey's expense.

In 1830, Serbia was made a self-governing state within the Turkish empire. A Serbian prince would rule with an assembly elected by the people. All but a few Turks left the country. Serbia had freed herself in bravery and blood, but most Slavs in the Balkans remained under foreign rule. Croatia, Slavonia, Slovenia and Dalmatia belonged to Austria. Bosnia, Hercegovina, and Macedonia belonged to Turkey. So did Montenegro, although the Turks were never able to establish control there. Even the sacred territory of Kosovo was still in Turkish hands. Throughout the Balkans, the eyes of the South Slavs turned toward free Serbia. Perhaps they too could win their freedom. Perhaps one day all the Slavs in the Balkans could join with Serbia in a single South Slav state.

During the long night of Turkish occupation, the situation in Bosnia and Hercegovina was even worse than it had been in Serbia. Although most of the inhabitants of Bosnia and Hercegovina were Serbs, the majority of them were not members of the Serbian Orthodox Church. Instead they belonged to the Bosnian Church, which believed in two gods, one good and one evil.

Members of the Bosnian Church were persecuted as heretics by all other Christians. To escape this persecution, many Bosnians readily became Moslems. The landowners were especially eager to convert when they realized that as Moslems they could retain their property and their privileges. Poorer Bosnians also converted, or returned to the Orthodox Church, and the Bosnian heresy died out.

Thus Bosnia divided along religious and economic

26

lines.   The landowners, now Moslem, were content to
let the Turks rule.   The majority of the people were
Orthodox Christian serfs, powerless to overthrow both
the Turkish invader and the local Moslem landlord.

In the nineteenth century, after 400 years of Turkish rule, feudalism still reigned in the two provinces.
Taxes were paid by those least able to afford them.
The tax collectors were local officials who, if they
did not get the amounts they demanded, did not hesitate to tie a serf to a tree, smear him with honey, and
leave him to the insects.   Yet the most inventive tortures could not force money from a man who had
none, and there were more taxes than any peasant
could pay.

There was a house tax, a land tax, a cattle tax, a tax
on certain flowers, a tax on every beehive.   Every
Christian family, rich or poor, had to pay a tax for
each male, whether an infant or a grandfather, in
place of his serving in the Turkish army.   Peasants
had to work without pay on public roads and on their
landlord's estates, and they were forced to lend their
horses or their children to the landlord whenever he
demanded them.   On top of all the taxes and forced
labors, the Bosnian serf had to give an eighth of all he
produced to the central government in Turkey.

In the fall of 1874, the crop was particularly poor
in the village of Nevesinje in Hercegovina.   Yet the
peasants were forbidden to harvest it until the tax collectors could come and claim their eighth.   But no tax

collectors appeared, while the grain rotted and the people starved.

The tax collectors did not come to Nevesinje until January of 1875. They rated the crop at far above its real value and demanded payment. But the peasants had been bled dry. They refused to pay. The tax collectors let loose bloodhounds, and those peasants who were caught were beaten and imprisoned. The rest fled to the surrounding mountains.

The Turks then sent in a commission to hear the grievances of the villagers. The peasants asked for the right to practice their religion, equal rights with Moslems before the law, protection against police brutality, lower taxes collected honestly and on time, and the abolition of forced labor. These are the usual pleas of an oppressed minority. But those who made them were the majority in their own country. What they lacked was the majority's right to rule.

The grievances were ignored. Instead, on July 1, 1875, Moslem fanatics butchered all the Christians they could find in Nevesinje. The other peasants came down from their hiding places in the mountains seeking revenge, and the battle was on. Fueled by centuries of anguish and persecution, rebellion flamed rapidly throughout Hercegovina and Bosnia.

It was only a peasants' revolt, but because so many nations had conflicting interests in the Balkans, it created hope or anxiety in every major capital in Europe. In 1876, the two small South Slav states, Serbia and Montenegro, came to the aid of their fellow Serbs and declared war on Turkey. Six months later they were joined by Russia, the largest Slav nation in the world. By 1878, Turkey was whipped. Russia forced her to sign a treaty that almost wiped out the Turkish empire in Europe and gave most of it to Bulgaria. Bosnia and Hercegovina were to be, like Serbia, independent states within the Turkish empire.

At this point, the other European powers intervened. In the days before air power, sea power was the key to greatness. Whoever controlled the Balkans controlled the adjoining seas. Therefore, the Balkan peninsula was much too important to too many nations to be left to its own people. England and France believed that the new Bulgarian state would be only a Russian puppet. This would make Russia too powerful, for it would give her control of a vital area of the Balkans and threaten the sea route to England's empire in Asia. The Austro-Hungarian empire did not want Bosnia and Hercegovina freed because it sought to add the two provinces to its own territory. Austria also feared that Bosnia and Hercegovina might someday be annexed by Serbia. A strong Serbia was a threat to Austria because she attracted the South Slavs within the empire.

Other nations also opposed the idea of independent South Slav states. Archaic empires, with their hordes of unrelated and quarreling peoples, seemed safer than vigorous new nations carved out of a common heri-

29

tage. Besides, the South Slavs had been treated as slaves for so long that some nations considered them suited for nothing else. "The Slavs were born to serve, not to rule," said an Austrian foreign minister. Because other Europeans were ignorant of the culture of the Serbs—their language, customs, music, and poetry—they concluded that the Serbs were uncultured, a barbaric people incapable of governing themselves. "Montenegro need have no port, only a little garden to grow cabbages and potatoes," said a British prime minister.

The major European powers refused to accept the Russian-Turkish treaty. Since the Tsar could not go to war with all of Europe he agreed to resolve the issues at a meeting in Berlin in the summer of 1878. At the Congress of Berlin, England, France, Germany, Austria-Hungary, Russia, Italy, and Turkey redrew the map of the Balkans. They swapped and bartered territories that were not really theirs to give or to take.

Serbia and Montenegro were recognized as totally independent states, but to keep them apart, a strip of territory that lay between them, the Sandžak of Novi Pazar, was given to Austria. Bosnian representatives went to Berlin to ask that their province be joined with Serbia or become an independent state within the Turkish empire. But the powers at Berlin were not interested in the wishes of the Bosnian people. Because it satisfied their own interests, the major powers

30

decided that Austria-Hungary should occupy and administer Bosnia and Hercegovina.

The date of the discussion was June 28, 1878, or Vidovdan. On the fatal anniversary of the battle of Kosovo Polje, the two provinces passed from one tyranny to another.

2 · The Broken Pot

Austria-Hungary was once described as "a broken pot held together with a piece of wire." The pot was misshapen, and the pieces did not fit together very well. They had little in common except the thin, tight wire that bound them all to the rule of the House of Habsburg.

During the Middle Ages, a German family, the Habsburgs, emerged as the rulers of a part of the Holy Roman empire called Austria. In the course of centuries, through marriages, treaties, and wars, the Habsburgs became the masters of central Europe. By the end of the nineteenth century, a Habsburg emperor reigned over a dozen different nationalities. Most Austrians were German, and most Hungarians were Magyars, but the empire also contained Czechs, Slovaks, Poles, Russians, Italians, Rumanians, Serbs, Croats, and Slovenes.

As with all ruling families, the Habsburgs produced strong men and weak ones, wise men and fools. In 1835 the throne passed to its rightful heir, an imbecile named Ferdinand. Ferdinand once said, "I am the emperor, and I want dumplings," and one historian has claimed this was the only sensible statement he ever made. Yet Ferdinand was permitted to reign until 1848, when, threatened by revolution, he abdicated in favor of his eighteen-year-old nephew, Franz Josef.

Franz Josef was to rule Austria for sixty-eight years. He was a very dedicated emperor and a very dull one. He worked each day from four in the morning until eight at night. Yet his long hours, like his long reign, accomplished little. In the wake of the French Revolution, the Napoleonic wars, and the revolutions that shook Europe in 1848, the continent stirred to the call of Liberty, Equality, Fraternity. But Franz Josef heard nothing. He saw the past better than he did the future, and he devoted his reign to the task of preserving the privileges and territories of the House of Habsburg.

During his long life, Franz Josef knew very little joy and much sorrow. His brother Maximilian was made emperor of Mexico by Napoleon III of France. This pleased Maximilian but not the Mexicans. The Emperor was executed by a Mexican firing squad, and his wife went mad.

Even though Franz Josef married for love, it brought him no happiness. When he was twenty-three he was captivated by his beautiful sixteen-year-old cousin Elisabeth, a wild, sensitive child, who preferred romping with her dogs and horses to being empress. "Yes, I do love the Emperor," she told her governess. "If only he were not emperor!" Franz Josef was a patient and devoted husband, but for Elisabeth, the palace was a prison and the Emperor was a bore. "Poor Franz has the soul of a sergeant," she said. The Empress traveled constantly, trying to flee from the life she hated. "I long for death," she wrote to her daughter. Four months later, on September 10, 1898, in Geneva, Switzerland, she was slain by an Italian anarchist. "Nothing has been spared me in this world," said Franz Josef.

The Emperor and his wife had four children, three daughters and one son. Crown Prince Rudolf was an ideal prince, handsome, charming, and romantic. He was also intelligent. He realized that the Austro-Hungarian empire could not survive unchanged in the modern world. When he was only fifteen years old he wrote, "The kingdom still stands, a mighty ruin, continuing from one day to the next, but doomed finally to fall."

Just as the kingdom was doomed to fall, Rudolf knew that he was doomed to inherit it. Someday he would sit on his father's throne. He would need the strength and the wisdom to make Austria into a modern state or preside over her death. Fearful of the challenge that awaited him, Rudolf tried to blot out the future with liquor, drugs, and women. But the fear remained. Finally, at the age of thirty, Crown Prince Rudolf committed suicide in a hunting lodge at

Mayerling. Franz Josef's epitaph for him was bitter. "My son died like a tailor," he said.

At the age of fifty-eight, the Emperor was without a son to inherit his crown. His nearest male heir was his brother Karl Ludwig, but since Karl Ludwig was an elderly and unworldly man, the role of heir apparent fell to his son, Franz Ferdinand. When Karl Ludwig died in 1896, there was no longer any question that Franz Ferdinand would one day be the emperor of Austria.

Franz Josef did not like his nephew and heir; he once called him a "dangerous madman." Almost no one liked Franz Ferdinand. His doctor described him as "one of the most hated men in Austria," and he was widely known as "the ogre."

Franz Ferdinand was born in 1863, 500 years too late. He was taught to believe in the twin pillars of medieval life, church and crown, but this was poor training for a man who would reign in the twentieth century. He also believed in the importance of the army, which he entered in his teens. He became a major general before he was thirty, and he would have been just another ill-tempered Austrian archduke of high military rank if not for Rudolf's suicide.

Unlike the gracious Rudolf, Franz Ferdinand was rude, miserly, and humorless. When he was twenty-nine he took a year's tour around the world. He disliked the United States, where he complained that the prices were too high, the service was poor, and people did not show proper respect for his royal blood. When he visited the Chicago world's fair he bought fifty-cent tickets to the circus and then protested because his seat was in the last row.

He kept a diary of his journey, and in it he set down his views on education. He believed in more training for the body and less for the mind. Boys should be taught discipline and duty, he wrote; this would produce suitable subjects for the empire. He once said of his own education, "We have learned everything and know nothing." Actually, he knew nothing because he had learned nothing. Art, science, mathematics, and languages were foreign to him. All his philosophical questions were answered for him by his religion. He read only those newspapers that supported his own views. As for the poets and the playwrights, he once complained, "Goethe and Schiller get their monuments, while many Austrian generals who have done more for our country are neglected."

Franz Ferdinand had only one hobby; there was just one thing he could do really well. He could kill. He was not so much a great hunter as he was a great marksman, for hunting implies using one's skills to search out the game, while Franz Ferdinand preferred to have it delivered to him. His doctor, Victor Eisenmenger, described a hunt in which sixty boars were penned up in an enclosure. One by one they were let out through a narrow gate to run past the hunters'

stands. The first hunter they passed was Franz Ferdinand. He killed fifty-nine and wounded the sixtieth.

When the Archduke hunted, beaters moved through
the woods in pear-shaped formation, driving the game
toward his tireless rifle. In this way he was able to
shoot 300 or 400 rabbits in a single day. On his
world tour, he hunted from the safety and comfort of
his moving train, and he traveled with his own taxi-
dermist.

Dr. Eisenmenger estimated that Franz Ferdinand
killed more than half a million specimens in his shooting career, including over 5,000 deer. On his best
day the Archduke slew 2,140 pieces of small game.
Other times his aim was not as good. Once he
missed the target and shot a beater instead.

All of his life Franz Ferdinand's health was frail
and in his early thirties he was so seriously ill with
tuberculosis that the court openly turned its attention
to his more amiable younger brother. The court
steward even cut the Archduke's allowance so it would
not be wasted on a dying man. Franz Ferdinand,
who was proud and sensitive, understood all and for-
gave nothing. "He suspected the worst of everyone,"
wrote Dr. Eisenmenger.

To the court's chagrin, Franz Ferdinand recovered.
But he became a hypochondriac, always fearing that
he had some serious illness. Perhaps he had. He
suffered from explosive fits of temper and once, in a
burst of anger, slashed open the upholstery in his rail-

way car with his sword. Some people believed that he was threatened by madness.

If he was not actually mad, he was almost insanely stubborn. Though he demanded that everyone else bow to the authority of the Habsburgs, he flouted it by choosing to marry beneath him. When he was in his mid-thirties, he began to make frequent visits to the castle of a distant cousin, the Archduke Friedrich and his wife, Isabella. It was assumed that he was courting one of their daughters. Then one day, after he had left the castle, a servant discovered that he had forgotten his watch. The servant brought the watch to Isabella, who saw there was a locket on the chain. She opened the locket, hoping to discover which of her daughters would be empress of Austria. To her horror, she found instead a photograph of her lady-in-waiting, Countess Sophie Chotek.

Sophie Chotek was one of seven daughters of a poor Czech noble. Franz Ferdinand met her at a ball in 1894, and for several years they corresponded secretly. When she became Isabella's lady-in-waiting in about 1898, Franz Ferdinand began to visit Friedrich's castle, not to court one of his cousins but to be with Sophie. With the discovery of the locket, the secret was revealed. Franz Ferdinand asked the Emperor for permission to marry. The Emperor said no. Franz Josef understood what his nephew chose to ignore. The Habsburgs retained their privileges, including the right to rule, only because their subjects still believed that one family is born better than another. If Franz Ferdinand brought someone of lower birth to the throne as empress, he would help destroy the myth on which monarchies rest.

Although Sophie was of noble blood, it was not noble enough. The Habsburg family laws listed the families that one might properly marry into, and the Choteks were not among them. Franz Ferdinand was advised that if he wanted to marry Sophie he would have to surrender his rights to the throne.

But Franz Ferdinand wanted both the throne and Sophie. "I have at last found a woman whom I love and who is suited to me," he told his doctor, "and now they are making the most unheard-of difficulties because of some trifling defect in her family tree. However, I shall overcome that." But it was not easy to overcome. No Habsburg could marry without the consent of the Emperor, and the Emperor would not consent. Franz Ferdinand finally asked his uncle if he would approve a morganatic marriage. That would mean his wife would not assume imperial rank, and his children would be unable to inherit the throne. Franz Josef felt this was not proper for a future emperor. Duty came before happiness.

The young man and the old one locked in stubborn conflict, and neither wanted to give way. Franz Ferdinand threatened he would go mad, or kill himself, or simply postpone his marriage until his uncle died. The threats did little good, but Franz Ferdinand won the support of three powerful allies, the Pope, the German Kaiser, and the Russian Tsar. Under considerable pressure, Franz Josef grudgingly agreed to a morganatic marriage.

Three days before the wedding, in front of the Emperor, the imperial family, and all the chief ministers and clergy of the Austro-Hungarian empire, Franz Ferdinand was forced to take a galling oath. The proud Archduke had to publicly proclaim that his marriage was not a proper one and that his children would have no right to the throne of the Habsburgs. The date of the oath of renunciation was June 28, 1900, Vidovdan.

Franz Ferdinand and Sophie Chotek were married on July 1. He was thirty-six years old; his wife was thirty-two. Neither his uncle nor his two younger brothers attended the ceremony.

The marriage was not the end of Franz Ferdinand's trial but only the beginning. Because he and Sophie were happy and in love, he was stung by every insult to his wife, and there were many. She could not sit beside him at official functions, and she had to walk behind the youngest archduchess in court processions. Yet these humiliations did not make Franz Ferdinand any more humane. He tried to prevent his youngest brother from marrying a professor's daughter and became enraged when the match was compared with his own. Sophie was not a commoner, he snapped; she was a countess!

Franz Ferdinand's bad health, bad temper, and bad luck aggravated an already angry disposition. His doctor called him "a good hater." He hated almost everybody: Jews, Protestants, freethinkers, Freemasons, liberals, courtiers, journalists, and Hungarians. Most of all he hated the Hungarians, whom he blamed for all the troubles of the empire.

He also had no great love for his uncle, the Emperor. Franz Josef was an old and inflexible man who did not like to hear unpleasant news and postponed all decisions for as long as he could. For all his many faults, Franz Ferdinand was neither stupid nor timid. He had faced many disagreeable facts in his lifetime, and he was not afraid to admit to himself that the Austro-Hungarian empire was falling apart.

Unlike Rudolf, who killed himself rather than inherit the throne, Franz Ferdinand could hardly wait. Everyone expected that there would be major changes when the Archduke was crowned, but no one knew exactly what they would be. Instinctively, people feared for their own positions. Franz Ferdinand's attitude toward his future responsibilities was illustrated when he said one day, "When I am commander-in-chief, I shall do as I wish. If anyone does anything else, I shall have them all shot."

Members of the Habsburg family and the nobility feared that when Franz Ferdinand finally became emperor he would renounce his oath of renunciation, make his wife the empress and his children his heirs, and take vengeance on them for all of the slights and insults.

The people feared him because he feared them. He believed in the absolute and divine right of kings. When the right to vote was extended early in the twentieth century, it was over his opposition. He said to a friend, "Even if unfortunately the times of feudalism and absolutism have passed, nobility with the emperor at the top . . . must act as the determining factor in all affairs of the empire." Clearly, with Franz Ferdinand at the top, the monarchy would be more autocratic, not more liberal.

The Hungarians feared that Franz Ferdinand threatened their unique position in the empire. Since 1867 Hungary had been roughly equal with Austria, partners in a dual monarchy, sharing one ruler and one army. The Hungarians rightly believed that Franz Ferdinand meant to change their role from partner to province, using force if necessary. Authority would no longer be divided; it would be centered in Vienna. Count Stefan Tisza, the prime minister of Hungary, warned that he would lead a revolt when Franz Ferdinand took the throne.

The Hungarians also suspected that Franz Ferdinand might try to change the dual monarchy into a triple monarchy. He would take millions of South Slavs under his rule and create a South Slav state within the empire, equal in importance to Hungary. Franz Ferdinand was seriously considering this plan.

Then in 1906 he attended army maneuvers in Herce-govina and Dalmatia and saw for himself the cold hatred of the Slavs for Austria. The crowds were so hostile that in one city the authorities offered to pay anyone who would cheer the Archduke.

"You know how matters stand here, and every sen-sible man knows it; only the government has no idea of it," he complained to an officer in Hercegovina. This journey, and many other incidents, convinced Franz Ferdinand that the Slavs would never be loyal subjects of the Habsburgs. He would not create a South Slav state that would one day rise up against him. Rather, he wanted the South Slavs to remain a subject people and "submit calmly and quietly to the culturally far superior Germans," as he wrote.

Thus the South Slavs had more reason to fear Franz Ferdinand than any of his other enemies. The others hated him because he threatened their rights and priv-ileges. The South Slavs hated him because he insured their enslavement.

3 · A Single Deed

When you live in a democracy you enjoy freedoms that are unknown in many parts of the world. You choose the men who make your laws. You choose the men who carry out your laws. You vote your leaders into office and, if they displease you, you can try to vote them out again.

The English philosopher John Locke once wrote, "No government can have a right to obedience from a people who have not freely consented to it." The people of Bosnia and Hercegovina had not consented to Austrian rule. They had simply been handed over by the Congress of Berlin in 1878. Austrian troops marched into the two provinces within two weeks after the congress ended. To their surprise, it took over 200,000 men three months to subdue the territory, even though the Austrians burned entire villages and shot civilian hostages. Over 5,000 Austro-Hungarian troops were killed or wounded; the Austrians did not bother to count the Bosnian casualties.

The businesslike Austrians wanted something in return for what it cost to have their troops and administrators in the two provinces, so they brought to market the rich natural resources of the area, mostly minerals and lumber. Industries were established. Roads were built, using the forced labor of the peasants. But everything the Austrians did in Bosnia and Hercegovina was for Austria; little was done to improve the wretched life of the natives. The feudal system remained. Taxes were ground out of the same serfs who could not pay them under the Turks. The peasants were kept poor and illiterate; they were easier to rule that way. When World War I began, nine out of every ten Bosnians could not read or write.

Although the villages were ignored, some schools were opened in the large cities, such as Mostar, the capital of Hercegovina, and Sarajevo, the capital of Bosnia. By the turn of the century these schools had become centers of opposition to Austrian rule. Forbidden by the authorities to organize openly, the students organized secretly. Even those student societies devoted solely to literature or philosophy had to meet in secret.

Many of the students were poor, hungry, and tubercular. They were the sons of serfs or poor traders who had the timeless dream of using education to better themselves. But they wanted to better their world as well, though they did not always agree on how this could best be done. Some were socialists, who wanted to redistribute property and authority. Others were anarchists, who wanted to destroy property and authority altogether. Most rebelled against the im-

45

morality of the world by being more moral, not less.

They wanted Bosnia and Hercegovina to be free of Austria, but they did not plot a revolution. With the patience of a people who had endured the Turks for over four centuries, they told themselves that the Austrian occupation was only temporary. The Congress of Berlin had given Austria-Hungary the two provinces only to occupy and administer on behalf of the Turks. Since they were not actually part of the empire, the Bosnians hoped the occupation would someday end. The students believed that by being educated, and by educating others, they were bringing the day of liberation closer.

Then in 1908, there was a revolution in Turkey and a vigorous new government took power. Fearful that Turkey might want Bosnia back, Austria evacuated the Sandžak of Novi Pazar but annexed Bosnia and Hercegovina. The two provinces became part of the Austro-Hungarian empire, and Europe almost exploded into war.

Serbia and Montenegro wanted to battle for their fellow Slavs, and all eyes turned to Russia. But the champion of the Slavs had her own problems. She was worn out by her recent war with Japan and threatened by internal revolution. The crisis was settled in March, 1909, when the German emperor, Wilhelm II, announced that a knight in "shining armor" stood by Austria's side. Too weak to battle both Germany and Austria, Russia backed down and war was averted, but only for five years. Russia and the South Slav states would not forget their humiliation. By openly seizing the territory, Austria had angered her worst enemy and united the South Slavs against her. She had also assured her destruction. When Bosnia and Hercegovina became part of the empire, it contained more Slavs than Austrians and Hungarians combined. In her greed, Austria had swallowed more than she could possibly digest.

Because of the continuing conflict over the Balkans, the situation in Europe was becoming highly inflammable. The only question was when it would go up in smoke. The older residents of Bosnia and Hercegovina, who had lived through the crises of 1878 and 1908, reassured each other. There would be a war soon enough—a European war. Austria would be defeated, and the South Slavs would be reborn in a new state. But now the young people refused to wait. After the annexation of Bosnia, they no longer believed that education and culture were the answers to oppression. They began to seek stronger weapons.

To celebrate the annexation, the Austrians held a special mass in the Orthodox cathedral in Sarajevo. The worshippers were asked to pray for the Emperor and the Habsburgs. Everyone obediently knelt except a group of boys from the Sarajevo high school.

The student answer to Austria was defiance. The secret societies jelled into a movement known as Mlada Bosna, or Young Bosnia. Young Bosnia was

47

an emotion rather than an organization. It is the name given to a generation of rebels, most of them high school students, representing many different strands of political and social thought but united in the desire for freedom.

In shabby rooms late at night, Young Bosnians, both men and women, met to discuss revolution. Influenced by both Serbian nationalists and Russian revolutionaries, they passed from hand to hand pamphlets and newspapers calling for political independence and economic equality. They knew what they wanted, but they did not know how to achieve it. Then a Young Bosnian law student named Bogdan Žerajić decided there was a way. When Bosnia and Hercegovina were annexed, Žerajić went to Serbia to fight in the war against Austria. When there was no war, Žerajić decided to take matters into his own hands.

In the spring of 1910, Emperor Franz Josef toured the two provinces. With a borrowed revolver in his pocket, Žerajić shadowed him for most of the trip. Yet Žerajić could not bring himself to fire at the old man. After Franz Josef left, Žerajić decided he would try again. This time his victim would be General Marijan Varešanin, the appointed governor of Bosnia and Hercegovina.

On the morning of June 15, in Sarajevo, Žerajić waited for Varešanin on the Kaiser Bridge, which spans the Miljačka River. As Varešanin's coach was about to turn from the Appel Quay onto the bridge, the student fired five times. Each time he hit the coach rather than the governor. With the sixth bullet, Žerajić killed himself.

Instantly, Žerajić became a hero. Legends sprang up about his life and death. It was said that Varešanin left his coach to kick and curse the dying youth. It was said that Žerajić's last words were, "I leave my revenge to the Serbs." Žerajić was buried secretly in a cemetery in Sarajevo, but Young Bosnians found his grave and covered it with flowers. When they passed the bridge where he had died, they removed their caps.

With Žerajić's act, Young Bosnia not only had a hero but a means. The means was the ancient one of tyrannicide—the slaying of the tyrant.

Tyrannicide is a custom as old as tyranny itself. In Greece and Rome the slayer of a tyrant was considered a hero, and monuments were raised to him. Seneca, the Roman philosopher, wrote, "No offering is more acceptable to God than the blood of a tyrant."

Philosophers and statesmen throughout the ages have defended the right of people to oppose tyranny. Benjamin Franklin proposed that the seal of the United States include the motto, "Resistance to tyrants is Obedience to God." Thomas Jefferson wrote, "The tree of liberty must be refreshed from time to time with the blood of patriots and tyrants."

Bogdan Žerajić had probably not read any of these statements, but he had other examples to guide him. One was that of Miloš Obilić, who slew Sultan Murad at Kosovo and became a Serb hero. More recently, in Žerajić's own brief lifetime, there had been some forty successful assassinations in different parts of the world. During the nineteenth and early twentieth centuries, assassination became a common political weapon. For by that time men had learned from the examples of the American and the French revolutions that tyranny could be overthrown. In a democracy, only a madman will commit political murder, for he can always hope to change his leaders by peaceful means. Where there is no democracy, there are no peaceful means. Where there are no peaceful means, desperate men may turn to violence.

There were eighteen separate attempts to kill King Louis-Philippe of France before he was forced off his throne in 1848. A French newspaper once commented satirically, "Yesterday the Citizen-King came to Paris with his superb family without being in any way assassinated." Others were not so fortunate, including a president of France, a king of Italy, and a prime minister of Spain.

The summons to kill oppressors was issued in the nineteenth century by a gentle Russian anarchist, Prince Peter Kropotkin, who wrote, "A single deed is better propaganda than a thousand pamphlets." Other revolutionaries like Karl Marx and Friedrich

Engels scoffed at individual acts of terror. They believed that only a broad-based political revolution could bring tyrants down. But the terrorists argued that the deed was needed to spark the revolution. "Terrorist activity, consisting in destroying the most harmful person in government, aims to undermine the prestige of the government and arouse in this manner the revolutionary spirit of the people and their confidence in the success of the cause," said one group of Russians. With this as their justification, they assassinated a tsar, three ministers, a grand duke, a governor, and a premier.

The Russian terrorists did not kill at random, nor did they approve of anyone who did. When United States president James Garfield was slain in 1881 by a disappointed office seeker, the Russian terrorists sent condolences to the American people. In their newspaper they wrote that because Americans are free to express their ideas, make their laws, and elect their president, assassination could not be justified. "Force can only be justified when employed to resist force," they said.

Bogdan Žerajić was deeply influenced by the Russian terrorists, and Young Bosnians were deeply influenced by Bogdan Žerajić. For over 400 years Bosnia had suffered conquest. Just as the feudal system survived there, so did the medieval ideals of individual vengeance and sacrifice. Most of the Young Bosnians were the sons of serfs, who had grown up in a land without justice or mercy. Hate for the foreign oppressor had been passed from father to son, along with the captive's concept that justice rests not in the law but in one's own hands.

Certain that nothing else would save their doomed land, the young rebels of Bosnia turned to the example of the deed. Their leading thinker, Vladimir Gaćinović, wrote a pamphlet about Žerajić called *The Death of a Hero*. The pamphlet became for Young Bosnia what the Kosovo ballads had been for their forefathers.

Cvetko Popović, one of the youths involved in the conspiracy against Franz Ferdinand, later wrote, "We read this pamphlet at meetings. . . . We knew whole passages by heart. The book had completely succeeded in its intention 'to instigate a revolution in the souls and minds of the young Serbs!' . . . These were not just words for us, but a program. . . . Each one of us had reached a decision to follow Žerajić. . . ."

The first student to follow Žerajić was a Bosnian Croat named Luka Jukić. Croatia was another South Slav province of the Austro-Hungarian empire; it was actually under Hungarian control. Early in 1912, the governor of Croatia, Count Slavko Cuvaj, adjourned the regional parliament and began to rule alone, with an iron fist. Students at the University of Zagreb, in the capital of Croatia, demonstrated in protest. Attacked by the police, they barricaded themselves in the university hall for a day and a half.

Sympathy demonstrations were held by youths in the empire's other Slav provinces: Dalmatia, Slovenia, Bosnia, and Hercegovina. The demonstrations spread to the high schools, and soon thousands of teenagers were on strike. In Sarajevo, the students burned a Hungarian flag, and one youth was shot in the head by the police. The purpose of the demonstrations was proclaimed in a pamphlet for which Jukić, a law student, wrote the preface. "We rose up against our oppressors," he said, "in order to convince them that they have not succeeded nor will they succeed with their method of occupation."

In the midst of the agitation, Jukić swore to other Young Bosnians that he would kill Governor Cuvaj. At about the same time a group of students in Dalmatia also decided to kill the governor. The plot against Cuvaj became a complex scheme involving revolutionaries in several Austrian provinces, as well as in Serbia. Jukić is said to have gotten his revolver from the secret Serbian society, the Black Hand.

On June 8, 1912, in Zagreb, Jukić fired at Cuvaj, who was in a car with his wife and another man. Jukić missed Cuvaj but hit the other man in the neck. The police set off in pursuit of the assassin. During the twenty-minute chase, Jukić fired four more times, killing one policeman and wounding two others.

Jukić was tried along with eleven youths, who were between fifteen and eighteen years old. All were accused of taking part in the conspiracy against Cuvaj.

When Jukić was found guilty and sentenced to hang, he cried out in the courtroom, "Down with tyranny!" Jukić was hailed as a new hero, and Cuvaj was warned by other students that they would finish what Jukić began. The Austrians struck back with arrests and imprisonments, but, fearing an uprising, they commuted Jukić's sentence to life imprisonment.

The young rebels now had two examples to follow, and they soon had a third. On October 31, 1912, another law student, Ivan Planinščak, shot at Cuvaj from a telegraph pole opposite the governor's residence. Planinščak missed and committed suicide.

The next assassin, Stjepan Dojčić, came all the way from the United States. Born in Croatia, Dojčić had sailed to America in his teens and found work in an automobile factory in Chenoa, Illinois. But the South Slavs in exile were often intensely nationalistic, and many of them formed societies for the purpose of liberating their native lands.

In October, 1912, Dojčić returned to Zagreb to try his hand at killing Governor Cuvaj. But having barely escaped two assassins, Cuvaj stayed out of sight. Dojčić spent months stalking his victim without success. Meanwhile, a new governor was named, Baron Ivo Skerletz. On August 18, 1913, in Zagreb, Dojčić shot Baron Skerletz, wounding him in the arm. At his trial Dojčić said, "Attempts against the lives of dignitaries is our only weapon. . . . If he were killed,

I would feel sorry for him as a man, but not as a governor."

The prosecutor blamed freedom of the press in the United States for corrupting Dojčić with "sinful ideas," and the youth was sentenced to sixteen years in prison. But the dream of the deed went on. On May 15, 1914, a month before Franz Ferdinand's visit to Sarajevo, a student named Jakov Šefer tried to kill Governor Skerletz and a visiting Austrian archduke. A Zagreb detective pounced on him before he could fire.

For every assassination attempted, many more were plotted. On November 22, 1912, police arrested a young barber who had intended to shoot the governor of Dalmatia the next day. In the summer of 1913, police arrested a Dalmatian student who was planning to go to Vienna to kill the heir to the throne. "Franz Ferdinand is the enemy of the unification of the South Slavs," the youth explained.

The South Slav students were bearers of a dream they could not legally realize and prisoners of a society they could not legally change. To make their dream of a South Slav state come true, and to create a rule of law that would be just rather than oppressive, the students had committed themselves to murder.

4 · Collision Course

The assassination attempts and the student demon-strations dramatically illustrated the hatred of the South Slavs for the Austrians. Austria-Hungary could have freed the South Slavs and helped them form their own state, but empires are always reluctant to dismember themselves. Instead, Austria's answer to the agitation was to throw students in jail, close the schools, further decrease the almost invisible freedoms permitted in the provinces, and accuse outside agita-tors. Unwilling to admit the problem was theirs, the Austrians blamed the disturbances on their small neighbor, Serbia. Free Serbia was a magnet that at-tracted the other South Slavs, who dreamed that she would serve as the core of a unified South Slav state. The only way to destroy the dream was to destroy Serbia.

But giant Austria was reluctant to attack tiny Serbia without cause. Russia or one of the other major pow-ers might intervene. During the closing decades of the nineteenth century, Austria had not been too con-cerned about Serbia. The Serbian monarchy was generally pro-Austrian and the country, lacking a seaport, was almost completely dependent on Austria to buy her goods. If Serbia became too much of a nuisance, the Austrians could strangle her by choking off her best market.

Then in 1903, the hated King and Queen of Serbia were murdered by a large group of Serbian officers. Almost 200 conspirators were involved in the muddled and gory assassination. Austria knew of the plot weeks before it was carried out, but did not warn the King. Austria had been even more deeply involved in the assassination of a Serbian ruler in 1868. Because his plans had threatened Austrian interests in the Balkans, Austria is believed to have arranged for his death. But nothing was done to punish her, for murder was an extension of foreign as well as domestic policy.

King Petar, who succeeded to the Serbian throne in 1903, was liberal and independent. When Serbia needed more arms, she decided to buy them from France. Austria objected; she wanted both the business and the opportunity to keep Serbia weak by controlling her weapons supply. Austria warned Serbia that if she went ahead with her plans, the empire would ruin her by putting a heavy tax on Serbian exports. Serbia defied Austria and bought the French guns.

Unwilling to declare war on the Serbian people, Austria-Hungary decided to declare war on Serbian pigs. Raising and marketing pigs was Serbia's major industry, and most of the animals were exported to

Austria. To punish Serbia, Austria raised the duties on all pigs and cattle coming from that country.

The Pig War turned out to be a disaster for Austria, not Serbia. The Serbians simply found new markets for their animals in other countries, while meat prices in Austria climbed. More important, Serbia had defied Austria and won. She was now free of Austria economically as well as politically. Serbia's triumph and Austria's humiliation gave new hope to the South Slavs who wanted to be free of the empire.

During the crisis that followed the annexation of Bosnia and Hercegovina in 1908, Austria became more determined than ever to go to war with Serbia. To justify the planned attack, fifty-three Serbs in Croatia were accused of conspiring with Serbia against the monarchy. They were tried for treason at Zagreb and thirty-one of them were found guilty. It was the first sham political trial of the century, for the documents used by the Austrian government to prove its case were forged. This was so obvious that Franz Josef was forced to pardon the defendants.

Forged documents were also given by the government to Austria's most important historian, Dr. Heinrich Friedjung, to write articles attacking Serbia and justifying war by attempting to prove that Serbs in Croatia were conspiring with Serbia to overthrow the monarchy. "Should it be ordained," wrote the historian, "that Austrian arms shall thoroughly purge Belgrade of the nest of conspirators . . . this would be a civilizing deed of great value. . . ."

Dr. Friedjung was sued for libel by the Croatian Serbs he had attacked. The Friedjung trial, like the treason trial, revealed that the Austrian government was forging documents to manufacture evidence against Serbia. As a result, the South Slavs in the monarchy became more pro-Serbian, and other nations began to wonder whether it was necessary for Austria to be so uncivilized in carrying out her civilizing deeds.

But outside opinion did not trouble the Austrian war party, which was led by General Franz Conrad von Hötzendorf, the chief of the General Staff. He was fully supported by his German counterpart, General Helmuth von Moltke. In 1909 Moltke wrote Conrad that if Austria attacked Serbia, Russia would come to Serbia's aid, and this would give Germany an excuse to attack Russia. The generals had World War I all mapped out long before it actually began.

In spite of Conrad's urging, Austria did not go to war with Serbia during the annexation crisis. Franz Josef opposed such a move. He was a peaceful man by nature, and he thrived on inaction. His heir, Franz Ferdinand, was also against the war, but for a different reason. He believed that Russia would fight for Serbia. "A war with Russia will finish us!" he once said. "Should the Emperor of Austria and the

59

Tsar push each other from the throne and open the road to revolution?" As far as he was concerned, Serbia was not worth the risk. "Suppose no one bothers us, and we can settle with the Serbians at our convenience?" he asked. "What will it get us? A lot more thieves and murderers and crooks, and a few plum trees."

Thus the anger roused by the annexation passed without war and the Balkans moved on to the next crisis. At the beginning of the twentieth century, one South Slav land still belonged to the dying Turkish empire. This was the southern portion of what had once been Dušan's empire. It included Macedonia and the battlefield of Kosovo Polje.

Macedonia is a dark and mystic land of many peoples: Serbs, Greeks, Albanians, Rumanians, Bulgarians. None of the South Slav nations suffered as long as Macedonia; it was the first area to fall to the Turks and the last to be freed. As Turkish power faded in Europe, several nations cast their eyes upon the area. The Habsburgs were still interested in a seaport on the Aegean. The Russian Tsar hoped to use Macedonia as a gateway to Constantinople. The German Kaiser saw it as a trade route to the East. The Serbians, Bulgarians, and Greeks each claimed Macedonia as a rightful part of their territory. And while everyone hungered over their land, the Macedonian people were alternately massacred by brigands, revolutionaries, Turks, and rival groups of nationalists.

After the revolution of 1908, Turkey was led by a group of Young Turks who promised reform and freedom, but who proved to be little better than the old Turks. Their rule began with a massacre of 30,000 Christians, and then they set out to restore order in Macedonia using torture, murder, pillage, and persecution.

At this point the Balkan states decided to unite against their common enemy, the Turks. Under Russia's guidance, Serbia, Bulgaria, Greece, and Montenegro formed a Balkan League. The members of the league asked the large European powers to join them in demanding reforms in Macedonia. The large powers, who had never felt the cut of Turkish oppression, told the league to be patient. Instead of presenting an ultimatum to Turkey, they presented one to the Balkan states. They would ask Turkey for reforms in Macedonia only if the league promised not to go to war.

Furious at this rebuff, the four Balkan nations declared war on Turkey in October, 1912. Four tiny, divided countries with a total population of 10,000,-000 challenged Turkey, whose population numbered 25,000,000 and whose armies had terrorized Europe for six centuries. The large powers, who preferred a weak Turkey in the Balkans to strong national states, sat back to pick up the pieces. To their horror, they had to pick up the wrong pieces. Within a month the Turks were virtually driven out of Europe. All they held were four cities.

Part of the Serbian army drove the Turks out of the Sandžak of Novi Pazar, while the main force headed for Skopje, once the capital of Dušan's empire. On October 22, the Serbians met the Turks in combat at Kumanovo, just northeast of Skopje. After three days of bitter fighting, the Turks retreated. With the victory at Kumanovo, the Serbians not only opened the way to their medieval capital but to the sacred field of Kosovo. When Serbian armies reached the plain where their freedom had been buried five centuries earlier, the soldiers fell to their knees and kissed the soil. Then they rose and walked softly over the land so their steps would not disturb the Serbian heroes who slept there.

Having united to drive Turkey out of Europe, the four Balkan nations immediately divided over the question of how to carve up the spoils. Austria and Germany persuaded Bulgaria that Serbia had cheated her, and the Bulgarians were only too happy to agree. On June 28, 1913, Serbian and Bulgarian officers dined together to celebrate the recovery of Kosovo on the anniversary of its loss. The following day the Bulgarians attacked the Serbians without warning.

Thus began the Second Balkan War. It lasted only one month. Serbia, allied with Greece and Rumania, crushed Bulgaria. In the peace treaty that followed,

Bulgaria and all the other Balkan nations recognized that most of Macedonia now belonged to Serbia.

As a result of the Balkan wars, Serbia and Greece almost doubled in size. More important, Serbia had freed Macedonia from the Turks. The South Slavs in the Austro-Hungarian empire now looked to her to free them as well.

"The heroic victories of the Serbian army were a real national baptism for the young," wrote Cvetko Popović. "They felt that Serbia was the natural center around which all the Slavs in the south of the empire should rally." Many Bosnian youths crossed the river Drina, which separates Bosnia and Serbia, to fight with the Serbians. Major Serbian victories were greeted in Bosnia with wild demonstrations. These soon turned into demonstrations against Austria. Police could not control the students and the army was called in. Infantrymen advanced on student mobs with rifles at the ready, and the cavalry rode their horses into the crowds. At night the Austrian cavalry patrolled the troubled streets. The governor of Bosnia and Hercegovina, General Oskar Potiorek, suspended the constitution of the two provinces and put them under military rule.

A frenzied Austria was still certain that the South Slav problem would disappear if only Serbia could be crushed. In November, 1912, during the First Balkan War, an Austrian official, instructed by his government to create an incident, claimed that he had been grossly mistreated by Serbian officers, but the story was a lie. In the spring of 1913, Austria almost went to war with Montenegro over Albania. Austria and Germany provoked Bulgaria into its sneak attack on Serbia in June of that year. When Bulgaria lost, Austria notified her allies, Germany and Italy, that she was going to attack Serbia and justify it as a defensive act. Both Germany and Italy replied that they would not support her, and Austria backed down, but not for long.

During the winter of 1913–1914, Austria twice tried to pick quarrels with Serbia, but Serbia refused to swallow the bait. She was so eager to avoid war that in 1909 and 1910 she offered to submit her disputes with Austria to the International Court at the Hague. Austria refused. In 1912, the Serbian prime minister offered to meet the Austrian prime minister to try to resolve their problems. The Austrian prime minister did not bother to reply. Early in 1914 the Austrian chief of staff, General Conrad, was writing to his German counterpart that war was imminent and asking, "Why are we waiting?"

While Austria was trying to start a war, the students in her conquered provinces were equally busy trying to start a revolution. The Austrians closed some schools and arrested some students, but every time they did, a new group of rebels was made. Cvetko Popović wrote that he did not become a revolutionary until he had spent four months in jail on suspicion of being one. He was not tried, because there was no evidence. But he spent four months in prison because some pamphlets the Austrians considered revolutionary were found in his room.

Before Austria's annexation of Bosnia and the Balkan wars, young men and women in Bosnia, Serbia, Croatia, and Slovenia had often been enemies. They were divided by ancient religious and national hatreds. But the two crises united the young South Slavs. Now their dream was to join their separate provinces in a single state.

By 1914, a vast network of revolutionary organizations blanketed the southern portion of the Austrian empire. Often the young rebels used youth hostels to cover their activities, and reduced train fares granted to hostelers helped revolutionaries travel about the monarchy preaching their cause.

But the students grew tired of words. The time had come again for deeds. Although none of the earlier assassination attempts had succeeded, the Young Bosnians still believed their problems would be solved by an *attentat,* the French word for an attack or assault on someone. "There was a general belief that attentats were the quickest means to revolutionize the people," wrote Popović. "The constant subject of discussion was the need for individual terrorist action. . . . Plans for attentats were contemplated against anyone who stood on the road to liberation from Austria-

Hungary. . . . Each one of us was ready to sacrifice himself."

In 1913, a group of Young Bosnians decided that their victim should be General Potiorek, the hated governor of Bosnia. "Not one but a hundred young men were thinking about that attentat," said Popović. The idea of killing Potiorek also occurred to Bosnian revolutionaries living in exile. A number of them met in Toulouse, France, early in 1914 to plan the assassination.

The task was assigned to Mehmed Mehmedbašić, a Moslem carpenter from Hercegovina. Mehmedbašić was given a dagger and a bottle of poison, to make the blade more deadly. With his weapons, Mehmedbašić set out for Bosnia. But on the train he suddenly became aware that the police were searching all the compartments. Panicking, he threw the dagger out the window and the poison in the lavatory. Later he discovered that the police were not looking for him but for a thief.

By the spring of 1914, Young Bosnia and old Austria were on a collision course. The Bosnians were looking for an Austrian to kill in order to spark a revolution. The Austrians were looking for an incident in order to start a war. Between January 1, 1913, and June 1, 1914, General Conrad had urged his government to go to war with Serbia no less than twenty-five times.

In this crackling climate the announcement was

made that Archduke Franz Ferdinand, heir to the throne of Austria-Hungary, would observe army maneuvers in Bosnia in June, 1914, and visit Sarajevo, the Bosnian capital. Although the announcement did not mention the date of the visit to Sarajevo, it would be June 28, Vidovdan, the anniversary of the battle of Kosovo.

5 · Six Are Chosen

A single thought flashed in the mind of almost every Young Bosnian. It has been claimed that at least ten different groups of nationalists planned to kill the Archduke, none aware of the others. Individuals who were not part of any group conspiracy also dreamed of the deed. One thing was certain: no matter who fired, Franz Ferdinand was not likely to leave Bosnia alive. When Mehmedbašić, embarrassed at his failure to kill Governor Potiorek, offered to try again, a leader of Young Bosnia told him to wait—bigger quarry was coming. Franz Ferdinand, the hunter, was about to become the hunted.

The Archduke seems to have decided to go to Bosnia for both political and personal reasons. The Habsburgs regularly toured their provinces; the Emperor himself had been to Bosnia in 1910, and it was time for another royal appearance. It was more than timely; it was mandatory. The army maneuvers in Bosnia and the Archduke's visit would remind the people that Austria had the strength and the determination to hold onto her provinces in spite of Serbia's victories in the Balkan wars. And perhaps it would revive the loyalty of the Croats and Moslems in the two provinces, most of whom tended to prefer Austria to Serbia.

Franz Ferdinand's personal reasons for the visit concerned his morganatic wife, Sophie Chotek. In the courts of Austria she was subject to insults and humiliation. On this tour she would be treated with full honors on Austrian territory, even if only in remote, rocky Bosnia.

Why June 28, Vidovdan, was chosen for Franz Ferdinand's appearance in Sarajevo, a hotbed of Serb sentiment, is unknown. For the Austrians, it may have been an oversight to schedule the visit on the bitter anniversary of the defeat at Kosovo. For the Serbs, it was an outrage. The defeat had finally been avenged by Serbia only two years earlier, during the First Balkan War. But the victory was not celebrated in 1913 because of difficulties with Bulgaria. June 28, 1914, would therefore be the first opportunity the Serbs would have to hail the liberation of Kosovo. A new oppressor had chosen that day to strut through Sarajevo.

When the newspapers announced Franz Ferdinand's visit, a group of Young Bosnians in Sarajevo decided to send the clipping to some Young Bosnians living in Belgrade, the capital of Serbia. Someone cut out the article, pasted it on a piece of paper, and put it in an envelope. Because mail was censored, no comment was made. None was necessary. A Young

Bosnian named Mihajlo Pušara typed a name and a Belgrade address on the envelope and mailed it. The name was that of Nedeljko Čabrinović. He had been chosen because it was believed that he owned a revolver.

Nedeljko Čabrinović was a nineteen-year-old typesetter. Born in Sarajevo, he was one of nine children. His father, who was a spy for the Austrian police, was a brutal man. The elder Čabrinović often beat his wife and children and once, when Nedeljko was fifteen, his father had him put in jail for three days.

Nedeljko dropped out of school when he was thirteen, and after trying several trades he learned how to set type for printing presses. He was barely in his teens when he became a revolutionary, and he was elected president of his guild of apprentices when he was fourteen. Since his home life was wretched, he was always either running away or being thrown out by his tyrannical father. His hatred for the older man soon turned into a hatred for all authority. Because the father was an Austrian spy, the son readily became a Serb patriot.

In 1912, during a printers' strike in Sarajevo, the police arrested Čabrinović. When he would not reveal the hiding place of one of the strike leaders, he was banished from Sarajevo for five years. This forced exile increased the youth's bitterness, for a foreigner had banned him from his own city. The ban

70

was lifted later that year, but after another quarrel with his father, Čabrinović went to Belgrade to live. He was working in the Serbian capital when he received the envelope with the announcement of Franz Ferdinand's visit.

At lunch that day Čabrinović showed the clipping to a friend of his, a youth named Gavrilo Princip. Princip had already read about the Archduke's plans in another newspaper. That evening the two youths met again and went for a walk. After a while they sat down on a park bench. Princip turned to Čabrinović and asked if he would join him in an attempt to assassinate Franz Ferdinand. "After a short moment's hesitation, I accepted this offer," Čabrinović later said. "We gave each other our word of honor, shook hands, and departed."

Gavrilo Princip was born on July 13, 1894, in Gornji Obljaj, a tiny hamlet in western Bosnia. The assistant parish priest carelessly recorded the date in the civil register as June 13, an error which was to mean life or death for Princip twenty years later. Princip's father was a peasant who earned extra money working as a postman. But life in the village was hard, and six of the nine Princip children died in infancy.

Because Gavrilo Princip had to help his father tend the sheep, he did not go to school until he was nine years old. When he finished primary school at the age of thirteen, his older brother, Jovo, decided Gavrilo should become a cadet in the military school in Sarajevo. This would give him a career, that of an officer in the Austrian army. But at the last moment someone persuaded Jovo that Gavrilo should not be made "an executioner of his own people."

Instead, Jovo enrolled his brother in a merchants school in Sarajevo, where he could learn how to make money. He also found him a room in the house of a widow named Stoja Ilić. Jovo did not know that Mrs. Ilić had a son, Danilo, who was an ardent rebel. The house was filled with revolutionary pamphlets, which Gavrilo Princip eagerly devoured.

After three years in the merchants school, Princip's friends convinced him that making money would be sinful. He transferred to a regular high school and had dreams of being a poet. In 1911, he joined some of the Young Bosnian secret societies. The following year he was expelled from high school for leading student demonstrations. He headed for Belgrade on foot. When he reached the soil of Serbia, he knelt and kissed it. In Belgrade he lived as a student and a revolutionary, supported by money sent by his brother.

During the First Balkan War, Princip twice tried to enlist in the Serbian forces. Both times he was rejected. "You are too small and too weak," said a Serbian officer, Major Vojislav Tankosić. Princip stared at the officer, his blue eyes burning with anger. There was more than one way to be a hero. With the announcement of Franz Ferdinand's visit, he saw his chance.

Balkan assassins make poor conspirators. They are too emotional, too gregarious, and they talk too much. No sooner had Čabrinović and Princip decided to kill the Archduke than they felt the need for a third accomplice. Princip invited his roommate, Trifun Grabež, to take part in the plot, and Grabež agreed. Eighteen-year-old Grabež was the son of a Serbian Orthodox priest from the village of Pale, a few miles east of Sarajevo. The year before, Grabež had been expelled from school for striking a teacher, and he had gone to Belgrade to continue his studies.

The newspaper clipping announcing the Archduke's visit had originally been sent to Čabrinović because his friends in Sarajevo thought he had a revolver. But he no longer had it, and besides, three assassins cannot fire one gun. Somehow, they had to find weapons. Through friends, the youths contacted Milan Ciganović, a Bosnian who had fought with Serbia during the Balkan wars. Ciganović went to Major Tankosić, the same Major Tankosić who had told Princip he was too small to fight for Serbia. A few days later Tankosić agreed to give the youths some weapons. He was acting not as an officer of the Serbian army but as one of the leaders of a Serbian organization, Union or Death. Its enemies called it the Black Hand.

The Black Hand was born during the angry months that followed Austria's seizure of Bosnia and Herce-govina. Many Serbians had been eager to go to war with Austria then, but Serbia, abandoned by Russia, had been forced to accept the annexation. The army was bitter, particularly the group of officers who had brought King Petar to power by assassinating his predecessor in 1903. Petar proved to be a wise and moderate man. For the officers, he was too moderate. They also disliked the Serbian prime minister, Nikola Pašić. They decided the country needed stronger hands—their own.

The leader of the dissidents was Colonel Dragutin Dimitrijević, whose nickname was Apis. Apis began to organize the Black Hand in 1909. Its key members were the assassins of 1903, but there were also many civilians in the organization. The seal of the Black Hand was engraved with a skull and crossbones, a dagger, a bomb, and poison. Members were initiated in a darkened room by a man wearing a black mask. They were sworn to secrecy or to death. Yet the aims of the organization were no secret. Its purpose was to unite all Serbs, wherever they might live, using revolutionary means. It opposed political rights, po-litical parties, and parliaments, and wanted a strong state run by the army and the church.

The men of the Black Hand and the boys of Young Bosnia were polar opposites. The Black Hand was an extremist right-wing society seeking a military dictatorship. Young Bosnia was an extremist left-wing movement seeking an end to political, social, and economic oppression. But both groups shared the desire to bring all South Slavs under the rule of Serbia. Both believed in terrorist activity to achieve this end. When Gavrilo Princip decided to kill Franz Ferdinand he did not hesitate to turn to the Black Hand for weapons, and Apis did not hesitate to give them to him.

The youths were given four pistols, six bombs, and some poison. Whoever succeeded in killing the Archduke was to swallow the poison so he could not be tortured into revealing the names of his accomplices. The bombs were flat, rectangular, and unsuitable for rapid action. The assassin would have to remove a cap, prime the bomb by striking the detonator against a hard object, and then wait twelve seconds for the explosion. Ciganović, their original contact with the Black Hand, and two other men showed the three youths how to fire the pistols. The lessons took place in a park in Belgrade, where Princip, using a tree trunk as a target, learned to shoot fairly well.

While he was training to be an assassin, Princip wrote a coded letter to his old friend, Danilo Ilić, in whose house he had lived in Sarajevo. Ilić, a twenty-four-year-old teacher and writer, was a leader of Young Bosnia and a member of the Black Hand. Princip told Ilić of the plot and asked him to find more assassins in Sarajevo.   He wanted to be sure that if one missed or lost his nerve, others would take his place.

In a city bursting with men and boys eager for a shot at the Archduke, and experienced enough not to miss, Ilić managed to find the three assassins least likely to succeed.   First he summoned Mehmed Mehmedbašić, the carpenter who had failed to kill Governor Potiorek several months earlier.   Ilić had promised Mehmedbašić that he would have a chance at bigger game and now he kept his word.

Having found one assassin who had lost his nerve on a previous attempt, Ilić then chose a pair of students who had never fired a gun in their lives.   The first was Vaso Čubrilović, a seventeen-year-old student at the Sarajevo high school.   In a moment of bravado one day Čubrilović boasted to a friend that he would kill Franz Ferdinand if only he had a weapon. The friend said he knew a man who would give him one.   The man was Ilić.

Čubrilović then recruited the sixth and last assassin. He was Cvetko Popović, an eighteen-year-old student at a teacher-training school in Sarajevo.   The two youths had spoken to each other only once, at a students' meeting.   But Čubrilović approached Popović because he had heard that the older boy had been imprisoned by the Austrian police.   In the feverish, unreal atmosphere of Sarajevo at that time, this was

76

considered enough to qualify someone to be an assassin.

On a rainy Friday in May, 1914, Čubrilović stopped Popović on the street and asked him if he had really been in prison and why. Popović explained that he was arrested because some revolutionary pamphlets had been found in his room. Čubrilović then asked Popović how he felt about Austria, Serb nationalism, and the other issues of the day, and it was soon apparent that the two youths held the same opinions.

Then Čubrilović began to talk about the army maneuvers and Franz Ferdinand's visit on Vidovdan. He and Popović agreed that the maneuvers were just rehearsals for an attack on Serbia and that Franz Ferdinand was an even greater enemy of the Serbs than his uncle, the Emperor.

"Well, it would be good to ambush him," said Čubrilović.

Popović did not know he was being tested but he replied feelingly, "Bosnia will bring a terrible disrepute upon herself—and especially the youth—if he is permitted to leave alive."

This was what Čubrilović wanted to hear. He looked directly at Popović and asked, "Would you be prepared to ambush him?"

"I would," was the immediate reply. "But what with?" Popović pointed to the mud beside the wet road. "You don't mean with this mud?"

"That's easy," replied Čubrilović, "if you really agree to do it." Then he told Popović what he knew, which was not very much. The Archduke was to be assassinated; Ilić would give them the weapons and the details later. Knowing no more than this, Popović solemnly promised to take part in the plot.

Years later, Popović wrote of this meeting, "All this is quite natural and understandable for anyone who knew at least something of the life of the youth [of Bosnia]. However, the judge-investigator and the presiding judge at the trial could not comprehend how it was possible that I immediately understood under Vaso's expression 'ambush' that he was speaking of an assassination. They could understand even less that we two, who did not know each other, at our first meeting reached the decision to take part in the heir-apparent's assassination! . . .

"This just shows how far they were from understanding our beliefs, our ideas, wishes, and feelings. For the same reason, they did not believe my statement that one could find not two but a hundred assassins among the youth in Sarajevo, and that it was only by chance that Ilić . . . had found Vaso [Čubrilović] and me."

6 · The Hunter Hunted

While Ilić was putting together a second team of assassins, the first three faced the problem of getting themselves and their weapons from Belgrade to Sarajevo, a distance of some 200 miles, without arousing suspicion. They not only had to evade the Austrian police but the Serbian police as well. They knew that the Serbian authorities did not want war with Austria and would stop them if they could. Again they turned to the Black Hand. The society had agents and sympathizers among the guards and peasants along the Serbian-Bosnian border, who helped slip people, pamphlets, and weapons into Bosnia unseen and unsuspected. Major Tankosić told the youths how to follow this underground route back to Sarajevo and who would help them along the way.

Princip, Čabrinović, and Grabež left Belgrade on the morning of May 28, heading west by boat along the Sava River. Each of them had two bombs strapped to his waist. In their pockets were the pistols, ammunition, and poison. From the first, Čabrinović frightened and infuriated his companions. He talked too much, too often, and to the wrong people.

Even though they were supposed to avoid strangers, particularly officials, he struck up a conversation on the boat with a Serbian policeman.

At their first stop, Princip had been told where to find an officer of the Serbian border guard who was a Black Hand agent. The officer told them the best place to cross the border and even arranged for them to get reduced train fares to their next stop. But they couldn't leave until morning, so they slept in a hotel in town, hiding their weapons in a stove.

At their second stop, the youths had to wait a full day until their next Black Hand contact could arrange for them to be taken across the border. Again Čabrinović talked freely to a stranger, and Princip and Grabež began to fear that he would reveal the plot. Because they had so much time to waste, they decided to send postcards to their friends and relatives. Čabrinović wrote half a dozen, several of which hinted that he had a heroic purpose in returning to Sarajevo. This made Princip angry, and there was a bitter quarrel. Princip told Čabrinović they would have to separate. Čabrinović could cross the border openly, using Grabež identification card; he couldn't use his own because he was too well known to the police as a troublemaker. At the same time, Princip and Grabež would cross secretly, carrying the weapons.

Čabrinović went on his way, and the other two youths continued along the underground route with

Princip's Bridge, as it looks today. The view is toward the corner where Gavrilo Princip stood when he fired.

Wide World Photos

Franz Ferdinand, Sophie Chotek, and their three young children, Ernst, Sophie, and Maximilian.

This photo was taken moments before the assassination. The car is just about to make the right turn around the corner where Princip waited.

Nedeljko Čabrinović, who threw a bomb at the Archduke and missed.

Danilo Ilić, who organized the plot in Sarajevo and was hanged.

Gavrilo Princip, at left, aged 16½, and at right, about 20, shortly after the assassination.

Trifun Grabež

Above, Veljko Čubrilović. Below, Mihajlo Jovanović. Both were hanged.

Vaso Čubrilović, Veljko's brother and the youngest of the assassins.

Cvetko Popović in November, 1918, after his release from prison.

Mehmed Mehmedbašić

The conspirators on trial. First row, left to right, Trifun Grabež, Nedeljko Čabrinović, Gavrilo Princip, Danilo Ilić, Mihajlo Jovanović. Cvetko Popović is seated in the second row, at the extreme right.

Ilić's house, as it looks today.

The surviving members of Young Bosnia standing before Princip's tomb on Vidovdan, June 28, 1967.

three bombs now strapped to their waists and revolvers in each pocket. On May 31 a Black Hand agent took them to an island in the middle of the Drina River. On the night of June 1, in a heavy rainstorm, they crossed into Bosnia. Their guides were peasants who were couriers for the Black Hand.

With only a brief rest, the youths walked through the mud and rain for twenty-one hours, until they reached the village of Priboj. Their peasant guides carried the weapons in a bag. In Priboj, their contact was a schoolteacher named Veljko Čubrilović. When Čubrilović saw the bag he said, "Are these weapons for the arrival of the heir apparent?" Princip replied, "If you want to know, they are." What Čubrilović did not know was that his younger brother, Vaso, was to be one of the assassins.

Princip asked Čubrilović to get them a horse and wagon to take them on to Tuzla, their next stop. After resting in Priboj that day they left late at night and arrived in Tuzla early the following morning. Their contact in Tuzla was Mihajlo Jovanović, a wealthy, middle-aged banker and businessman. Princip asked Jovanović if he could take the weapons to Sarajevo for them; Jovanović hesitated. Then Princip asked Jovanović to hold the weapons until he or someone else came for them. Jovanović agreed to do this. He put the weapons in a cardboard box and hid the box in the base of his dining table.

In Tuzla, Princip and Grabež met Čabrinović, who

had arrived two days earlier. A Black Hand agent had taken him to a Serbian frontier post, where a guard passed him through on Grabež identification card. Then Čabrinović walked to the Austrian side of the border and entered Bosnia without difficulty.

As usual, Čabrinović talked with everyone in sight. In Tuzla he met an Austrian detective who was a friend of his father's. The detective asked Čabrinović where he had been and the youth obligingly informed him that he had just come from Serbia. When the three youths took the train to Sarajevo on the night of June 3, the detective was aboard. Again Čabrinović chatted with him. The detective asked Čabrinović if he knew the name of that strange-looking youth in the next compartment. Čabrinović replied that the boy's name was Gavrilo Princip. Then Čabrinović and the detective discussed Franz Ferdinand's trip. This time it was the detective's turn to be helpful. When the youth asked for the exact date of the royal visit to Sarajevo, the detective replied that it would be June 28.

Princip, Čabrinović, and Grabež arrived in Sarajevo on the morning of June 4. The trip from Belgrade had taken eight days. The weapons, however, were still in Tuzla, underneath Jovanović's dining table.

When they reached Sarajevo, the three youths went their separate ways. Čabrinović moved back with his parents and got a job in a local printing plant. He told everyone who would listen that he had just come from Belgrade with two friends. Grabež returned to his family's home in the village of Pale, visiting Sarajevo from time to time for the latest news of the plot. Princip, who thought he was the most clever of the conspirators, made the most serious error. He went to live in his old room at the house of Danilo Ilić's mother. Since everyone who came to Sarajevo had to be registered with the police, Princip dutifully reported his address to the local authorities. When the time came, the police would have no trouble linking the two chief conspirators.

Princip had so little money that he had to borrow from Ilić to pay his rent. A week before Vidovdan he got a job doing some clerical work. To avert police suspicion he avoided his Young Bosnian friends and spent his evenings in cafes with rowdier companions.

It was Danilo Ilić who finally brought the weapons to Sarajevo. On June 14, he went to Tuzla and asked Jovanović to take them to a railway station a few stops away. Jovanović packed the arms in a sugar box, wrapped the box in newspapers, and tied it with string. He took the box to the station where he was supposed to meet Ilić, but Ilić was nowhere in sight. Jovanović covered the box with his coat and left the weapons in the waiting room while he went to find Ilić. While he was gone, the station cat dozed on the box. When Ilić still didn't appear, Jovanović left the box with a friend, a local tailor.

Ilić finally arrived and claimed the weapons. To

avoid being stopped by the police he made his way back home using the most indirect route possible. When the weapons were safely in his house he put them in a wooden box under Princip's bed.

Ilić told Princip that he had arranged for three more assassins, but he did not reveal their names. Mehmedbašić was at his home in Stolac, Hercegovina, waiting to be summoned. The two local students, Čubrilović and Popović, were in Sarajevo, also waiting. Popović later described his thoughts as the day of the deed approached.

"The whole night, after my assent to the assassination, I spent thinking and dreaming of it. The next day I was a completely different man. I reconciled myself to the thought that I would live till Vidovdan only. From that time on I looked at everything around me in a different way.

"I stopped studying my school subjects. The newspapers, which I had read regularly, no longer interested me. Friendly teasing, which would once have made me burst out in anger, I now regarded from a height. . . . Generally I turned everything into a joke and I was in a very good mood.

"There was only one thought that could make me serious: the thought that we would not succeed and that we would disgrace ourselves. . . . I felt that the honor of the nationalist youth was at stake and if we disgraced ourselves we would blot a whole generation. . . .

"I used to meet Vaso [Čubrilović] from time to time. Ilić told him that besides us two there would be four more 'waiting' for the heir apparent. At the beginning I did not believe that and I thought that Ilić said this in order to encourage us both, for what should he do with six assassins!"

But there were indeed six assassins, or one for each bomb. Having made the arrangements, however, Ilić began to have doubts about the whole plot. To spark a revolution, you need a people ready for revolt. Perhaps it would be better to organize a political movement in Bosnia and Hercegovina first, and kill later, or not at all. An assassination at the wrong time would benefit no one except the war party in Austria.

Princip did not agree. He felt the time to kill Franz Ferdinand was now. Besides, he later admitted that "a certain morbid yearning for it had been awakened in me."

Doubts about the assassination had also struck the Black Hand. On June 15, Apis and Major Tankosić told the central committee of the organization in Belgrade that they had armed a group of Bosnians who planned to kill the Archduke. The members of the committee, fearful of the consequences to Serbia, violently objected and Apis sent a message to Ilić telling him to stop the plot. But Princip would not be stopped. He and Ilić spent the second half of June debating the issue. Instead of distributing the weapons to the other assassins, Ilić kept them under Princip's bed while a decision was being reached.

Princip never wavered; he wanted to kill Franz Ferdinand. It was Ilić who was torn by doubts. Then, at the end of the month, Ilić made up his mind to go ahead with his part of the plot. There is evidence that suggests that Apis defied the orders of the Black Hand and secretly sent a messenger to Ilić telling him to proceed as planned.

On Friday, June 26, Ilić sent a telegram to Mehmedbašić telling him to come to Sarajevo. On Saturday, June 27, the day before Vidovdan, Ilić finally gave the weapons to Čubrilović and Popović, neither of whom had ever fired a gun in his life. Popović not only could not shoot, but he could barely see. He was so nearsighted that he could not recognize a friend across the street, and he was too poor to buy glasses. With a gun in his hand, Popović was more of a danger to himself than he was to the Archduke.

Ivo Kranjčević, a friend who knew about the plot, offered to lend Popović his glasses, but Popović refused them. He had never worn glasses in his life; if he wore them on Vidovdan the police might suspect something. Anyway, in his daydreams, Popović had already determined how he would kill his victim. "Vaso [Čubrilović] would stand next to me," he decided, "and when his bomb caused confusion and stopped the heir apparent's car, I would have the opportunity to come up and throw my bomb and after that we would start shooting from our pistols. The last bullet we would use to kill ourselves, and in order to be on the safe side we would swallow potassium cyanide a few moments before throwing the bombs."

That Saturday, fantasy turned into fact. At about two in the afternoon, Popović and Čubrilović met at a cafe. Ilić arrived a little later, his face pale, his pockets stuffed with newspaper. Sitting in the cafe, he poured out some grains of poison, wrapped them in strips of newspaper, and gave a packet to each of the youths. Then they walked to a park on the outskirts of Sarajevo. Strolling through the park, Ilić gave Čubrilović a bomb and a pistol. Further on, when they were out of sight in a tunnel, Ilić took out the second bomb. He unscrewed the cap and showed the students the detonator. Hit it against a hard object, said Ilić, count to ten, and throw it. It will explode two seconds later.

Ilić screwed the cap back and gave the bomb to Popović. He then took out the second pistol, showed the youths how the safety lock worked, and fired one bullet into the tunnel wall. The shot echoed loudly and Ilić said, "Where this hits, no balm would help." Then he gave the gun to Popović.

The lesson was over. Čubrilović and Popović had received all the training they would get for their part

87

in the most important assassination of the century. When they left the park, they walked along the Appel Quay. Ilić showed them where to stand along the Archduke's route. He told them that if they could not fire the first time Franz Ferdinand passed, they should find new places and shoot him on the return trip.

After the meeting with Ilić, Popović went directly to his room. "Although I had been preparing a whole month for the next day," he later wrote, "still I was very excited. I examined closely both the bomb and the pistol and imagined what would happen the next day. I even did some kind of practice. I pretended to be throwing the bomb with my right hand and then I quickly passed the pistol from my left to my right hand and pretended to be shooting."

Mehmed Mehmedbašić, who had come to Sarajevo in response to Ilić's telegram, received his weapon Saturday evening. Ilić gave him a bomb and told him how to use it. The three remaining assassins had agreed to meet in a cake shop at eight o'clock the following morning to complete their plans. The sensitive, erratic Čabrinović knew that Princip did not believe he would carry out his part of the plot. On the evening of June 28 Čabrinović wrote to a friend, "Tomorrow is Vidovdan and we shall see who is faithful and who is unfaithful. Do you remember the great oath of Miloš Obilić?"

Čabrinović was also thinking of a more recent tyrannicide. Four years earlier Bogdan Žerajić's unsuccessful attempt to kill the governor of Bosnia had ignited a generation of rebels. Now the rebels paid their respects to their mentor. That Saturday Čabrinović visited Žerajić's grave in the cemetery in Sarajevo. Later that evening, Ilić did the same thing. Near midnight, Princip came. The assassins were ready. All they needed was their victim.

Franz Ferdinand had departed for Bosnia and Hercegovina with doubts and fears. He knew how restless the people were under Austrian rule and he knew how unpopular he was. Between 1902 and 1914 three unsuccessful attempts were made on his life, and there were rumors of at least a dozen other plots. In 1911, Franz Ferdinand had planned to go to Bosnia, but changed his mind after being advised to stay away. When his visit was announced in 1914, officials in Bosnia, Serbia, Vienna, Budapest, and Berlin warned of the dangerous mood of the people. "Serbian youth is ready for anything," said one report.

The warnings had their effect. Early in June, Franz Ferdinand met with the Emperor and said he would prefer not to attend the Bosnian maneuvers because of his bad health. The Emperor replied, "Do as you like."

But Franz Ferdinand's pride overcame his fear and he decided to go. "I am inspector general of the Austro-Hungarian armed forces," he told his children.

"I must go to Sarajevo." Anyway, assassination plots were an occupational hazard for any ruler; his uncle, the Emperor, had once been stabbed in the head. "Our life is constantly in danger," the Archduke said. "One has to rely upon God."

Franz Ferdinand and his wife began their journey on June 23. Their three children, two boys aged eleven and nine and a girl of thirteen, remained in Austria. On the day of his departure, Franz Ferdinand gave his valet a gold watch and asked that if anything happened to him the servant remain to care for the Duchess and their children.

The trip began ominously. First, the Archduke's private railway car caught fire before Franz Ferdinand could board it. It had to be uncoupled from the train and left behind. "Well, that's a promising beginning for this trip," said Franz Ferdinand. "Here, our car burns down; there, they will throw bombs on us."

Later in his journey, the Archduke was given another parlor car, but the wiring system failed and had to be replaced by flickering candles. "What do you think about these lights?" the Archduke said to his secretary. "Just like in a grave, isn't it?"

Franz Ferdinand and his aides traveled by train and battleship to Hercegovina while his wife went directly to Bosnia by train. They were reunited on June 25 at the resort of Ilidže, a few miles south of Sarajevo. That evening they made a surprise visit to the marketplace in Sarajevo, where Moslem craftsmen still sit crosslegged in their stalls, hammering exquisite designs into copper. The crowds were friendly, and there were no incidents.

The following two days Franz Ferdinand attended army maneuvers about ten miles west of Ilidže. General Potiorek, the governor of Bosnia and Hercegovina, was in charge. When the maneuvers were over, Franz Ferdinand sent a telegram to the Emperor praising the troops and saying, "Tomorrow I shall visit Sarajevo and leave in the evening."

While the Archduke observed the maneuvers, his wife visited the schools and orphanages of Sarajevo. She was never in any danger as long as she was alone. In all their fevered plotting against Franz Ferdinand none of the assassins had ever thought of shooting his wife. To them, harming a woman was shameful and degrading.

On the evening of June 28, while several of the assassins were visiting Žerajić's grave, there was a lavish dinner for Franz Ferdinand at Ilidže. Thus far the trip had gone well, and the Archduke and the Duchess were pleased. Sophie Chotek said to a Bosnian politician who had warned them of the dangers of coming to Sarajevo, "You were wrong after all."

"Your Highness," he replied, "I pray to God that when I have the honor tomorrow night of seeing you again, you can repeat those words to me."

7 · June 28, 1914

The program for June 28 had been carefully arranged. Franz Ferdinand and his wife would arrive in Sarajevo by train. Near the station there would be a rapid troop review and then the couple would be driven up the Appel Quay to a reception at the town hall. After the reception the Archduke would go on to the national museum in Sarajevo. He would meet his wife again at the konak, the governor's residence, where they would have lunch. In the afternoon there would be a sightseeing tour. Dinner would be at Ilidže at seven and two hours later the royal train would begin the return journey to Austria.

At about eight o'clock that morning, Ilić, Čabrinović, and Grabež met in a cake shop, as planned. Before leaving home, Čabrinović had divided his possessions among his relatives. He gave his mother his pocket knife and his watch and he gave his grandmother and one of his sisters most of his money. Tearfully he told the girl he would never see her again.

At the cake shop he recovered well enough to eat three pastries before Princip arrived. The conspirators went to the back room and Princip gave Čabrinović a bomb, which he stuck into his belt. Princip also gave Čabrinović some poison wrapped in paper, but he did not give him a gun. There were only four pistols for six assassins. Čubrilović and Popović already had two; Princip and Grabež were to have the others. Čabrinović did not get one because Princip did not believe the blustering, boastful youth would have the courage to fire.

After leaving the shop, the vainglorious Čabrinović met a friend and suggested that they go to a photographer's shop to have their picture taken, which they did. Čabrinović later explained, "I thought that posterity should have my picture taken on that day."

While Čabrinović was obliging posterity, Grabež went with Ilić to the schoolteacher's house and got the last bomb and revolver. However, Ilić forgot to give Grabež his portion of poison, which remained wrapped in a piece of paper in Ilić's pocket.

All of the assassins were on the street, fully armed, long before the Archduke came. Princip passed the time walking about the Appel Quay with two friends, one of them the son of Sarajevo's attorney general. Popović, who had refused to wear glasses because they might make him look conspicuous, was stalking through the streets in a heavy, black wool cape on a blazing summer day. Yet neither the cape, nor the bulging weapons, nor the assassins aroused any suspicions.

Bosnia was a police state, with strict controls over its citizens, yet no one could have been less effective than the men who were supposed to be protecting Franz Ferdinand. For every error the assassins made, the authorities made two. It was impossible to move about the country freely, yet three of the assassins were able to cross the border, bringing weapons in with them, without being caught. Two of the youths had crossed illegally; one had used someone else's identification card. But when Princip and Čabrinović registered with the police in Sarajevo, no one bothered to find out that Čabrinović had entered Bosnia on Grabež card and that Princip had never legally entered at all.

The police were even more careless when it came to actually guarding the Archduke. Sarajevo was honeycombed with Austrian spies and informers, but they seemed to be the only persons in the city who did not know about the plot to kill Franz Ferdinand. The assassins had spoken freely enough, and on the eve of Vidovdan, Čubrilović let his friends feel the weapons in his pockets as they sat in a shop eating ice cream.

When Emperor Franz Josef had visited Sarajevo in 1910, two rows of soldiers shielded him from his subjects as he rode through the streets. Over 200 persons considered potentially dangerous were imprisoned and others were kept under house arrest. When Archduke Franz Ferdinand came the danger was far greater, but only about thirty-five persons were arrested. The assassins were not among them, even though five of them, and Ilić, were known agitators. No soldiers lined the streets for Franz Ferdinand, even though thousands were nearby for the maneuvers. Instead, only some 150 police and detectives guarded the Archduke on his long route through the city. They mingled freely with the crowds, but so did the assassins.

When Franz Ferdinand rose on Sunday morning, June 28, he dictated two telegrams. One was to his secretary. The other was to his children, telling them that all was well and that he would see them Tuesday.

At 9:00 A.M., Franz Ferdinand and Sophie Chotek attended mass in a room at their hotel. At 9:25 a special train took them from Ilidže to Sarajevo, where Governor Potiorek was waiting. The Archduke quickly reviewed the troops at the camp opposite the station, then he and his wife took their places in the procession that was to go up the Appel Quay to the town hall. It was now about 10:00 A.M.

There were six cars. The first was for the special detectives who were assigned to the Archduke. But after their chief and three local police officers entered the car, the driver pulled away, leaving the other men behind.

The mayor of Sarajevo and the chief of police rode in the second car. Franz Ferdinand and Sophie were in the third car, which had its top folded back so the visitors could be seen. Franz Ferdinand sat on the left. He wore a general's uniform with a high-collared blue tunic and black trousers with red stripes down the sides. His officer's helmet was decked with green feathers. Sophie Chotek sat at his right in a white silk dress with a red sash. General Potiorek sat in front of Franz Ferdinand on a folding seat, and Lieutenant Colonel Count Franz Harrach sat next to the driver. Behind the Archduke's car came three others bearing various aides and officials.

Shortly after 10:00 A.M., the procession reached the first assassin, Mehmed Mehmedbašić. Mehmedbašić, who had lost his nerve in an earlier attempt against Potiorek, now lost it again. He later explained that just as the cars approached, a policeman came up behind him. He decided that if he removed the bomb from his belt, the policeman would seize his arm before he could prime and throw it, the plot would be revealed, and the other assassins would have lost their chance to kill the Archduke. While all this was passing through his head, the cars, naturally enough, passed also, and it was too late to do anything. The first assassin had failed.

The next assassin was Vaso Čubrilović, one of the two local students. He was armed with a gun and a bomb, but he did nothing. He later explained that he did not fire for fear of hurting the Duchess. "I did not expect to see her at his side," he said. The other local student, Cvetko Popović, was farther up the quay. He later wrote,

"As the fateful moment was approaching I again became excited. . . . Suddenly the crowd started to murmer and everybody pushed to the front lines on the edge of the pavement. I remained alone in front of the tobacco shop, because I wanted to hit the bomb against the wall. . . . I carefully put the potassium cyanide, which I had wrapped in cigarette paper, into my mouth. Then, under the cape, I took the bomb in my right hand and the pistol in my left hand. I was in a special mental state, in a sort of hypnosis. I was continuously repeating below my breath: Now, they are coming; now, they are coming. . . .

"The noise of the cars reached my ears and the crowd started to shout: 'He's coming!' The first car passed at a rather high speed. Now they are coming! I was waiting for the explosion of Vaso's bomb. Suddenly a weak [sound] was heard. I looked in the direction it came from and I noticed a lean, tall young man standing on the opposite side, at a lamppost. . . . The rolling crowd closed my view, and the continuous cheers, 'Long may he live! Long may he live!' told me that the heir apparent was approaching. At this moment the second car passed and immediately afterward a bomb exploded."

At the trial, Popović explained his own inaction by saying, "I had no courage. I do not know what happened to me." Of the first four assassins, only one did what he came to do. The weak sound that Popović heard was that of a bomb being primed against a lamppost, and the tall young man he saw across the street was Nedeljko Čabrinović.

Čabrinović, the sentimental braggart whom Princip would not even trust with a gun, was the first assassin to act. As the cars approached, Čabrinović turned to a detective. "In which car is His Majesty?" he asked. Instead of watching the crowds, the detective was excitedly watching the procession. He replied that the Archduke was in the third car. Čabrinović removed the bomb from his belt and primed it against the lamppost, but he could not wait ten seconds because Franz Ferdinand's car was already passing. He aimed at the green feathers and tossed the bomb underhand into the narrow street.

Those few uncounted seconds saved the Archduke's life. The driver of the car saw an object hurtling toward him and pressed his foot on the gas. The bomb fell on the folded roof of the car, but it was not ready to explode. As the Archduke raised his arm to protect his wife, the bomb bounded off the roof and into the street. It exploded beneath the wheels of the fourth car.

Čabrinović threw himself on the ground, swallowed the poison, and lunged over the embankment into the

98

Miljačka River, twenty-six feet below. If the poison didn't kill him, the water would. But the poison failed and so did the river, which was at low tide. Čabrinović was fished out alive by the police. When they asked him who he was he replied, "I am a Serb hero."

At the sound of the explosion, the Archduke ordered his car to halt. He sent Count Harrach back to see who had been injured. Two officers were bleeding; one of them, Lieutenant Colonel Erich von Merizzi, had been hit in the head by a bomb fragment. About twenty bystanders had also been hurt. Sophie Chotek had been grazed in the neck, and there were three small holes in the Archduke's car. But no one had been killed.

The first two cars, with the police and the mayor, had continued on their way to the town hall, unaware of what had happened behind them. While Count Harrach was checking on the injuries in the fourth car, Franz Ferdinand sat unguarded in a car parked in the middle of the street, yet no one fired. Three of the assassins had lost their nerve and the remaining two did not know what had happened, even though they were only a block or two away.

Princip later said that when he heard the bomb explode he thought that one of the others had succeeded. He saw Čabrinović being led away by the police and for a moment considered killing Čabrinović and then himself to keep the secret of the conspiracy, but he decided not to. He walked a few steps to the Lateiner

Bridge and there he learned that the attempt had failed. Knowing the Archduke's return route, Princip looked for a good place to stand for a second try. The last assassin, Grabež, who was waiting opposite the town hall, never attempted to fire.

When Franz Ferdinand was satisfied that his injured aides were being cared for, he said, "The fellow [Čabrinović] must be insane. Gentlemen, let us proceed with our program." The party continued up the Appel Quay to the town hall, passing two more assassins unharmed.

On the steps of the town hall, there was to be a short welcoming ceremony. The mayor of Sarajevo bravely began his prepared speech. "Our hearts are full of happiness on the occasion of the most gracious visit with which Your Highnesses have deigned to honor the capital of our land, and I consider myself happy that Your Highnesses can read in our faces the feelings of our love and devotion——"

The Archduke exploded harshly. "Mr. Mayor," he said, "what is the good of your speeches? I come to Sarajevo on a friendly visit and someone throws a bomb at me. This is outrageous!"

The Duchess spoke quietly to her husband and calmed him down. Finally he said, "Now, you can get on with your speech."

After the mayor delivered his greetings, the Archduke was scheduled to reply. But the aide who carried the speech had been in the damaged car, and he had not yet arrived. When the manuscript was finally delivered to the Archduke it was covered with blood. However, Franz Ferdinand read it and added a few words thanking the people of Sarajevo for "their joy at the failure of the attempt at assassination."

After the speeches, the official party went inside the building. Sophie went upstairs to a reception of Moslem women and children, while Franz Ferdinand stayed downstairs. He was nervous and angry, and he stormed about the room making bitter and sarcastic comments. "You mark my words!" he said. "The chap will probably, in good old Austrian style, be decorated with the Order of Merit instead of being made harmless. Today we shall get a few more little bullets."

No one laughed. The Bosnians in the room stared at him in awe, because they knew that what he said was true. Someone who was there later told the writer Rebecca West, "We were all silent, not because we were impressed by him, for he was not at all our Bosnian idea of a hero. But we all felt awkward because we knew that when he went out he would certainly be killed. No, it was not a matter of being told. But we knew how the people felt about him and the Austrians, and we knew that if one man had thrown a bomb and failed, another man would throw another bomb and another after that if he should fail."

The only man in the room who seemed to think that Franz Ferdinand was safe was the man in charge of security arrangements, General Potiorek. Franz Ferdinand taunted the governor with being unable to preserve order and he demanded, "Do you think more attempts are going to be made against me?" Potiorek expressed his regrets for the incident and assured the Archduke that the danger was over. According to some accounts Potiorek is supposed to have said, "Do you think that Sarajevo is full of assassins?"

In spite of Potiorek's optimism, the officials discussed changing the program to protect Franz Ferdinand from another attempt. There was no longer any real question that his life was in danger; the problem was how to get him out of Sarajevo alive. Potiorek suggested that Franz Ferdinand cancel his visit to the museum and go directly to the konak or leave for Ilidže at once, not stopping anywhere. Someone else suggested that the Archduke stay where he was until all the people were ordered off the streets and troops were brought in to escort him out of town.

Potiorek objected vehemently. He would not bring in troops to line the streets because they were not in dress uniform. Because ceremony came before safety, the Archduke had to die.

The final decision was the Archduke's. He decided he wanted to go to the hospital to visit his wounded aide, Merizzi. After that he would go on to the museum and then to the konak. Everyone knew what the return route would be because it had been published in the newspapers. He was scheduled to drive about two blocks down the Appel Quay and then make a right turn opposite the Lateiner Bridge onto Franz Josef Street. Potiorek now recommended that instead of making the turn the Archduke's party drive directly down the quay at high speed. This would outwit any more assassins who might be waiting along the announced route.

Sophie Chotek had not been scheduled to go to the museum with her husband, and he told an aide to drive her to the konak or back to Ilidže. But when the aide told her this the Duchess replied, "As long as the Archduke shows himself in public today I will not leave him." When the Archduke urged her to reconsider she said firmly, "I will go with you to the hospital."

At about 10:45 A.M., the Archduke and the Duchess walked down the seven steps of the town hall and reentered their car. Franz Ferdinand again sat on the left, with his wife at his right. Potiorek sat in front of them, but this time, instead of sitting next to the driver, Count Harrach mounted the left running board to shield the Archduke with his body. Since the first assassin had struck from the side of the street that bordered the river, Harrach assumed that any other attack would come from the same side. It did not occur to him or anyone else that there might be an assassin on the other side of the street.

The cars sped rapidly down the Appel Quay. When they reached the Lateiner Bridge, the first car, instead of going straight ahead, made the right turn onto Franz Josef Street. No one had bothered to tell the driver that the route had been changed. The driver of the second car followed the first, and the third car, with the Archduke, swung around the corner.

Startled, Potiorek shouted, "What is this? Stop! You are going the wrong way! We ought to go via Appel Quay!" The driver had to stop in order to back up. Standing on the pavement only a few feet away was the only assassin still waiting for the Archduke, Gavrilo Princip.

After failing the first time, Princip had crossed the street to the corner opposite the Lateiner Bridge. He knew that Franz Ferdinand was supposed to make a right turn there, and so he waited in front of Moritz Schiller's delicatessen. If the chauffeurs had been told about the new route and had continued down the quay instead of making the turn, Princip would not have had a second chance.

Princip recognized Franz Ferdinand as soon as the car halted and began to back up slowly, but he hesitated when he saw the Duchess. He had only an instant to think. He wanted to throw his bomb, but it was on the left side of his belt, with the cap still on. It would have been impossible to remove it, unscrew the cap, prime the bomb, and fling it with the crowd pressing around him.

Instead he raised his pistol. A detective saw him

and reached for his arm, but at that moment a Young Bosnian kicked the detective in the knee. The youth was Mihajlo Pušara, who months before had sent the envelope with the announcement of Franz Ferdinand's visit to Čabrinović in Belgrade.

Princip fired.

"I aimed at the heir apparent," he told an investigator shortly afterward. "I believe that I fired twice, perhaps more, because I was so excited. Whether I hit the victims or not, I cannot tell, because instantly people started to hit me."

For a few moments, no one knew exactly what had happened. Both the Archduke and his wife were so tightly corseted that they remained bolt upright in their seats. But Potiorek ordered the driver to go directly to the konak, on the other side of the Miljačka River.

As the car was backing up to cross the Lateiner Bridge, a stream of blood spurted from the Archduke's mouth. Count Harrach, who could not save Franz Ferdinand because he was standing on the wrong side of the car, bent over and wiped the blood with his handkerchief. When Sophie saw this she cried, "For God's sake! What has happened to you?" Then she fell from her seat with her face between the Archduke's knees.

Harrach thought she had fainted from the shock. But Franz Ferdinand cried, "Soferl, Soferl, don't die. Live for our children."

Then his head sank forward. Harrach seized him by the collar to keep him upright. "Is Your Highness in great pain?" he asked. "It is nothing," said Franz Ferdinand. He repeated this six or seven times, each time more faintly.

The Archduke and the Duchess were carried into the konak. Sophie was probably already dead. A bullet had torn through the side of the car and into her side. Franz Ferdinand died about fifteen minutes later. A bullet had pierced his jugular vein.

The most important moments in history are often the most baffling. Great events do not always make good sense. Franz Ferdinand should never have died in Sarajevo. There was a plot against him, but it was inept, and the assassins were only bumbling boys. There were many times during the day when a change of plan would have saved his life, but a series of unrelated blunders put him on the only street corner in Sarajevo where an assassin still waited.

When Princip saw the Archduke he was not ready to fire. His weapons were still in his belt. He was surrounded by a crowd. He was standing off balance and he was hardly an expert shot. He fired without aiming and with his head turned away from his target. Yet both shots were fatal, and because of them the history of the world changed forever.

8 · Ultimatum

When Franz Ferdinand and Sophie Chotek were dead, they finally got the protection they needed. Soldiers lined the streets three deep when the bodies left Sarajevo on June 29. Soldiers carried the coffins to the hearses, and soldiers led the funeral procession to the railway station.

In Vienna, the reaction to the news of the assassination was shock rather than sorrow. Franz Ferdinand had too many enemies to be mourned. The eighty-four-year-old Emperor was quoted as saying, "The Almighty cannot be provoked! A higher force has restored that order which unfortunately I was not able to maintain." In other words, God had punished his willful nephew for the disastrous marriage. Franz Josef was much more direct in speaking of the assassination to his youngest daughter. "For me it is a great worry less," he said.

Count Stefan Tisza, the Hungarian prime minister who was ready to revolt when Franz Ferdinand took the throne, is supposed to have said, "God has wanted it this way, and we must be grateful to God for *everything*." An Austrian politician wrote in his diary,

"Perhaps . . . God meant to be kind to Austria by saving it from this emperor."

The two coffins returned to Vienna by train and boat. In the Austrian capital, the Archduke and the Duchess faced the same hostility in death as they had in life. The court officials who hated Franz Ferdinand and despised his wife for her lower birth now took vengeance on the unresisting corpses. Franz Ferdinand was to be buried with his ancestors in the Capuchin crypt in Vienna, but the court chamberlain, Prince Alfred Montenuovo, ruled that this honor was too great for a duchess. Sophie was to be buried separately in a crypt which Franz Ferdinand had built at his castle of Artstetten. But Franz Ferdinand had anticipated this, and he had directed in his will that he was to be buried at Artstetten with his wife.

Montenuovo was forced to bow to the will, but then he ruled that Sophie was too low in rank to lie in state beside her husband. The new heir to the throne, Franz Ferdinand's nephew, Karl Franz, protested to the Emperor, and Montenuovo was overruled. Nonetheless the fanatic prince was determined to deny Sophie Chotek all honors, even if it meant denying them to the Archduke as well. He ordered the special train bearing the bodies to arrive in Vienna late at night so there could be no ceremonial procession from the station, and no one of importance was to meet the coffins. But defying Montenuovo, Karl Franz came to the station with a number of nobles and officers and led an unscheduled procession to the chapel.

The following morning, July 3, the public was permitted to view the coffins for only four hours. Sophie's coffin was lower than her husband's, to indicate her lower rank. Atop Franz Ferdinand's coffin were a crown, a general's hat and sword, and the Archduke's medals—symbols of his royal rank. Atop Sophie's coffin were a pair of white gloves and a black fan—symbols of a lady-in-waiting.

Funeral services began at 4:00 P.M. and ended exactly fifteen minutes later. The Emperor was present, but showed no sign of caring. The service was notable not only for its brevity but for the absence of foreign dignitaries. The heir to one of the most important thrones in Europe was being buried, and yet no other kings or princes were present. The Austrian government had specifically asked them not to come. The official reason was that the Emperor was in poor health and could not receive visitors. The actual reason was that the Austrian hawks were already planning to use the incident to destroy Serbia. They were afraid that if foreign heads of state met in Vienna for the funeral they might resolve the incident without resorting to war.

At 10:00 in the evening, the bodies were taken from the chapel to the railway station to begin the journey to Artstetten. Because Sophie would be with

Franz Ferdinand, the implacable Montenuovo decided that the Archduke could not depart with the military honors due him as head of the armed forces. Local garrisons did not have to line the streets unless they wanted to, and the archdukes and the nobility were asked to stay home.

The Austrians had little enough love for Franz Ferdinand when he was alive, but Montenuovo's savage etiquette won great sympathy for the corpse. Troops voluntarily lined the streets and over 100 members of Austria's ancient and noble families chose to follow the horse-drawn hearses to the station. There, Karl Franz waited with all the archdukes of the House of Habsburg to bid his uncle a final farewell.

Montenuovo, who had too much to do with the funeral arrangements in Vienna, refused to have anything to do with them once the bodies left the capital. The train that took the coffins to the station nearest Artstetten arrived at 2:00 in the morning. Additional services were to be held in the square outside the station, but as the train arrived, it was greeted by a violent thunderstorm. Someone decided to hold the services in the waiting room, but by the time all the honor guards and the mourners had gathered around the coffins, there was no room for the local dignitaries. So while services for the slain heir to the throne were being held in the waiting room of a country railway station in the middle of a stormy night, the local dignitaries, having nowhere else to go, went to the station's refreshment stand, which was conveniently open, and drank.

After the services, the coffins were placed on horse-drawn hearses. Since the court refused to make any provision for the mourners, they had to follow in ancient, rented taxicabs. The road was uphill, and when the vehicles sank into the mud, the mourners had to get out and walk.

In this manner, the procession made its way to the ferry that was to take them across the Danube River. It was still dark and stormy, and in midriver, several of the hearse horses bolted at the sound of a thunderclap. One of the coffins almost slid into the river.

In the morning, the bizarre funeral finally ended at the castle of Artstetten. Franz Ferdinand had had a crypt dug beneath the church there so he and his wife could be together in death. He was pleased with the crypt but not with the entrance. "It makes too sharp a turn," he had said. "Awkward bearers will knock off a corner with the coffin. Then I shall turn in my grave."

Franz Ferdinand was right. As the soldiers made the sharp turn into the crypt, the edge of the Archduke's coffin struck the wall and a piece of stone broke off. But there was no sound from the coffin. Franz Ferdinand was no longer able to comment on anything that was done to him or in his name.

Having shown no respect for the Archduke in Vienna, the Austrians now began to show an excess of it elsewhere. In Sarajevo, more than 200 leading Serbs, none of whom had anything to do with the conspiracy, were arrested immediately after the assassination. By the end of July, 5,000 Serbs throughout Bosnia and Hercegovina were in prison. The Austrians selected peasants at random, tortured them, and then hanged them in the prison courtyard beneath Princip's and Čabrinović's window. Altogether, about 150 Serbs in the two provinces, both men and women, were hanged in retaliation for the Archduke's murder. The assassins would receive a trial, but the peasants, who had never known Princip, who had never known anything but Turkish and Austrian oppression, were executed without a trial, without evidence, without guilt.

But Austria was not content simply to hang a few Serb peasants and priests. For years the war party had sought a reason to go to war with Serbia. General Conrad, the Austrian chief of staff who had called for war with Serbia twenty-five times during the previous seventeen months, described the assassination as a "godsend." "This is not the crime of a single fanatic," he argued. "Assassination represents Serbia's declaration of war on Austria-Hungary. . . . If we miss this occasion, the monarchy will be exposed to new explosions of South Slav, Czech, Russian, Rumanian, and Italian aspirations. . . ." An Austrian diplomat in Belgrade wrote, "Serbia must learn to fear us again."

To punish Serbia for the assassination, Austria first had to prove that she was responsible for it, and this presented several problems. First, Franz Ferdinand would never have been killed if he had been guarded properly. Austrian newspapers bitterly criticized Potiorek for the poor security arrangements, but he was never reprimanded by the government. To even suggest that Austrian officials had been careless might lessen the alleged guilt of the Serbians.

Second, the assassins were not Serbians. Five of them were Bosnians. The sixth, Mehmedbašić, was a Moslem from Hercegovina.

Third, Serbia would not be likely to provoke an incident that might lead to war at a time when she was having serious internal problems. Colonel Apis and the army were challenging the government for control of Macedonia. King Petar, who was seventy-three years old, had resigned four days before the assassination and appointed his son Alexandar as prince regent. Under pressure from Apis, Prime Minister Pašić had resigned on June 2. Parliament had been dissolved on June 24, and new elections were scheduled for August 1.

Serbia was not only in the midst of a severe political crisis, but she was worn out by the two Balkan wars. Since she had a peasant army, she would not choose to go to war in the summer because experience had shown that the soldiers would simply go home in the fall to harvest their crops. The Serbians were so unprepared for war that the commander of their armies was on vacation—at an Austrian resort.

It was true that the assassins had gotten weapons and other assistance from a Serbian society, the Black Hand. But the Black Hand hated the Serbian government as much as Austria did. Besides, who had helped the assassins was not really the point. Franz Ferdinand was killed because Bosnia wanted to be free of Austria. Punishing Serbia would not solve Austria's problem.

Nonetheless, Austria was determined to have her little war. It was easier to fight than to admit her mistakes. The hawks wanted to attack without warning. The courtesy of a declaration of war was for civilized nations, and the Austrians did not consider the Serbians to be civilized. But their first obstacle was Emperor Franz Josef, who had doubts about the whole thing. His nephew's death had solved his greatest problem, and he saw no reason to punish anyone for it. He was also reluctant to end his long reign with a war and possibly a revolution.

The hawks then tried to enlist the support of Count Tisza, Hungary's prime minister. Tisza rejected the suggestion of a surprise attack as a "fatal mistake." One did not "start a great war under the most unfavorable circumstances," he said. To make certain that circumstances would be favorable, he recommended that the monarchy first make sure it had the support of Germany and Bulgaria.

Traditionally, the three great emperors of Europe had been allies; Austria, Russia, and Germany had to preserve their ancient autocratic systems against the terrors of democracy. But Austria knew that in a war with Serbia, Russia would probably support the Serbians. In that case, Austria wanted to be sure that Germany would keep her promise of 1909, when the Kaiser said he would stand by Austria's side in shining armor.

At the beginning of July, Franz Josef wrote Kaiser Wilhelm that Serbia had to be isolated, weakened, and "eliminated as a political factor in the Balkans." On July 5 Wilhelm replied that Vienna could count on Germany's "faithful support." That same day Wilhelm ordered his military leaders to start preparing for war, but not to "attract political attention."

At the same time, in Vienna, the indefatigable General Conrad was again trying to persuade the reluctant Franz Josef to agree to go to war. The Emperor protested that Russia would intervene. If that happened, Conrad said, Germany would support Austria.

"Are you *sure* of Germany?" asked the Emperor.

"If . . . Germany is on our side, shall we then make war on Serbia?" asked Conrad.

"In that case, yes," replied Franz Josef.

When the Kaiser's promise of support reached Vienna, a joint council of ministers convened on July 7. The Austrian foreign minister, Count Leopold von Berchtold, informed the assembled dignitaries that they could rely on Germany. True, there was some danger that Russia might enter the war, but for that reason, the sooner Austria attacked, the better. If she moved quickly and Germany stood firm, Russia might back down before the knight in shining armor as she had done in 1909. For Russia had grave political problems and, if she went to war, she risked a revolution. Besides, she was still in the process of building key railroads. By Austrian calculations, Russia would not be ready for war until 1916. It was therefore urgent to deal with Serbia promptly. The longer Austria delayed, the better prepared Russia would be.

Having deliberately chosen to go to war and refused to consider any alternatives, everyone at the meeting now agreed that they had no choice; war was unavoidable. All except Tisza supported the idea of a surprise attack. The Hungarian prime minister did not like the idea of Austria-Hungary seeming to be the aggressor, even if she were; this would only unite all Europe against the monarchy. He suggested that Austria first make demands of Serbia. If Serbia agreed to them, Austria would have won a great diplomatic victory. If Serbia rejected them, Austria would have justification for war. And if there was going to be a war, Tisza cautioned, it should be to punish Serbia and not to absorb her. A small war, with limited

116

aims, would be less likely to cause Russian intervention. Besides, he did not want any more South Slavs in the empire.

The others at the meeting agreed with Tisza that an ultimatum should be sent to Serbia. But they made it clear that it must be so strong that Serbia could not possibly accept it. They did not want a diplomatic victory; they wanted war.

To justify the assertion that the assassination was the work of the Serbian government and to justify a war already decided upon, Austria decided to hold an inquiry in Sarajevo. A high Austrian official, Friedrich von Wiesner, went to Sarajevo on July 10 to examine the evidence gathered by the local investigators. Three days later Wiesner telegraphed his conclusions to Vienna.

"There is nothing to show the complicity of the Serbian government in the direction of the assassination or in its preparations or in the supplying of weapons," he wrote. "On the contrary, there is evidence that would appear to show such complicity is out of the question. . . ."

Since Wiesner's report disproved rather than supported the Austrian case, Berchtold suppressed it and went ahead with his plans. An ultimatum to Serbia was to be delivered at 5:00 P.M. on July 23. Serbia would have only forty-eight hours to reply, which would give her no time to consult with any other nation. The hour was chosen because the President of

France, who was visiting Russia, would have set sail by then and would not have the opportunity to discuss the situation with his ally, the Tsar. He would be at sea, both literally and figuratively, during the critical forty-eight hours.

When the Germans later checked and discovered that the French President might not be gone at that hour, they warned Vienna and delivery of the note was postponed until 6:00 P.M. Both Germany and Austria considered no detail too trivial to guarantee that war would be inevitable.

9 · War

The Austrian minister in Belgrade delivered the note promptly at 6:00 P.M. on July 23. Serbia was totally unprepared for the ultimatum. Her political leader, Nikola Pašić, was not even in the capital. He was campaigning in what had been the Sandžak of Novi Pazar, and a messenger had to be sent out on horseback to find him.

The Austrian note claimed that "the confessions of the murderers" proved that the crime had originated in Belgrade. All that three of the youths had actually said was that they were living in Belgrade when they decided to kill Franz Ferdinand. The note called on Serbia to condemn and prohibit all anti-Austrian activities within her borders and made ten specific demands:

1. that Serbia suppress all anti-Austrian publications;
2. that she dissolve all anti-Austrian societies;
3. that she eliminate from the Serbian school system anything that served to promote anti-Austrian propaganda;

4. that she dismiss all officials or officers guilty of such propaganda;

5. that she accept "the collaboration in Serbia" of Austro-Hungarian officials in suppressing this anti-Austrian activity;

6. that she open a judicial inquiry into the assassination and permit Austro-Hungarian representatives to take part in it;

7. that she arrest two of the men who helped the assassins obtain their weapons, Major Vojislav Tankosić and Milan Ciganović;

8. that she halt the smuggling of arms and explosives into Bosnia and dismiss the Serbian frontier guards who helped three of the assassins cross the border;

9. that she explain "unjustifiable" language used by high Serbian officials after the assassination;

10. that she notify Vienna without delay that all these measures had been carried out.

Serbia had just forty-eight hours to reply. The Austrian minister in Belgrade was instructed by his government that there could be no extension of time and no negotiations. If the note was not accepted unconditionally, he and his staff were to leave Belgrade at once.

The following morning Austria delivered copies of the ultimatum to Germany, Russia, France, England, Italy, and Turkey. The Austrians enclosed a letter appealing for the sympathy "of all civilized nations" in their effort to eliminate Serbia as a menace to the peace of Europe. But several nations questioned who was the real menace. The harsh time limit was obviously intended to prevent Serbia from seeking a third party to mediate the quarrel, and the Austrian demands were excessive, if not impossible. The British foreign secretary commented that he "had never before seen one State address to another independent State a document of so formidable a character."

In Belgrade, Pašić and other Serbian leaders met with Prince Regent Alexandar. On July 24 the Prince telegraphed Tsar Nicholas II of Russia. He said that Serbia would try to meet the Austrian demands, but that some of them would require new laws, which could not be passed within the time limit. Expecting an attack by Austria, he appealed to the Tsar for help. Russia, which did not want war, urged Serbia to concede everything. But the Russian telegram did not even reach Belgrade until the time limit had expired.

Desperately eager to avoid war, Serbian officials reined in their pride and composed a submissive reply to Austria. They denied Serbia's guilt and essentially bowed to all of the demands except for the sixth. Serbia would open a judicial inquiry, but she could not permit Austro-Hungarian representatives to take part in it since this would violate her constitution and her criminal code. If this did not satisfy Austria, however, Serbia was willing to have the question referred to the International Court at the Hague. This was the third time since the Bosnian crisis of 1908 that Serbia had offered to submit her disputes with Austria to international arbitration. Each time Austria refused.

Pašić personally delivered Serbia's reply to the Austrian minister at two minutes before 6:00 P.M. on July 25. By 6:30 the Austrian minister was on his way back to Vienna.

Everywhere but in the Austrian capital Serbia's reply was believed to be acceptable. Even Kaiser Wilhelm scribbled on his copy of the Serbian note, "By it every reason for war is removed. . . ." In a later letter he wrote, "On the whole the wishes of the dual monarchy had been met. . . . The few reservations . . . can . . . be cleared up by negotiation. But the capitulation has been proclaimed . . . and puts an end to every reason for war." But the erratic Wilhelm's pacifism dried with the ink. Almost immediately Germany reassured Austria that she would support her if Russia intervened when Serbia was punished.

And Serbia would be punished; Austria had decided that even before the Serbian reply was received. A legal memorandum had been prepared which said that even if Serbia accepted the ultimatum without a single reservation it would still be unacceptable because she

122

would be unable to present proof, within forty-eight hours, that she had done everything demanded of her. Absolutely nothing the Serbians could have done or said would have prevented Austria from going to war with them.

Only one man in Austria still had some doubts about the war. He was old Franz Josef, who wanted to die in peace. And it almost seemed that he might have his wish. So many offers of mediation were made, especially by England, that Berchtold, the Austrian foreign minister, became desperate. He decided he had to start the war before anyone could stop it. The Emperor was told that Serbia had rejected the ultimatum, which was hardly true. "So it has come after all," the old man sighed. Then he added hopefully, "Well, the rupture of diplomatic relations does not yet mean war."

The foreign minister grew frantic in the face of the Emperor's relentless pacificism. On July 27 Berchtold told Franz Josef that Serbian troops had already begun the war by firing on Austrian troops from steamers in the Danube River. "Hostilities, therefore, have actually developed," he said.

It was an outright lie, but it worked. That night the Emperor said to General Conrad, "If the monarchy must go down, it shall at least go down decently." On the morning of July 28, exactly one month after Franz Ferdinand's assassination, Franz Josef signed the declaration of war against Serbia.

The tortuous route that led from the shots of Sarajevo to the guns of August had been mapped long before Princip fired. The nations of Europe were knotted into such interlocking rivalries and alliances that they were like a chain of firecrackers. If one exploded, the others had to follow.

For years a European war had been only an incident away. Everyone knew it; the statesmen had prepared their speeches and the generals had prepared their plans. The English spoke of "when the big war comes on," and the German chief of staff had said as recently as June 1, "We are ready, and the sooner the better for us."

The assassination of Franz Ferdinand provided the spark, and the firecrackers exploded one by one. None of the nations involved was entirely innocent of responsibility for making "the big war come on." Austria felt she had to destroy Serbia or lose her empire. Russia did not want to go to war with Austria, but if she left Serbia to her fate, she would forfeit her position as champion of the Slavs and the Balkan peninsula would be wide open to Austrian influence.

Austria and Germany had an alliance in which each agreed to come to the aid of the other in a war with Russia. But Russia had an alliance, too; she and France had agreed to come to each other's aid in the event of war with Germany. Germany had known for years that when the war came, she would have to fight on two fronts. Her generals had decided that if they attacked France first, with the bulk of their strength, the French could be destroyed before large, lumbering Russia even mobilized her armies. To strike France where it would do the most harm, Germany had decided to attack through Belgium, even though Belgium was a neutral nation. If Germany violated Belgium's neutrality, she risked war with England.

On July 29, the day after Austria declared war on Serbia, Russia began partial mobilization of her armies. Germany, which was already mobilizing, demanded that Russia cease. On July 30, the Tsar ordered full mobilization. On July 31, England asked France and Germany to guarantee Belgium's neutrality in the event of war. France agreed; Germany would not say. That same afternoon, Germany asked France if she would go to war as an ally of Russia. France replied that she "would consult her own interests."

On the afternoon of August 1, Germany openly ordered full mobilization and declared war on Russia. That same night German troops marched into neutral Luxembourg and seized the railways, which they needed for an invasion of Belgium. On August 2, Germany demanded that Belgium permit her to send troops in to protect herself from a French attack. If Belgium refused, she would be regarded as an enemy and suffer the consequences. Belgium refused.

On August 3, Germany declared war on France, claiming that France had already attacked her. Like the alleged Serbian attack on Austria, this was a lie used to justify action already decided upon. At this point, England's leaders were still divided. Some wanted to enter the war as an ally of France; others wanted no part of it. Then, on the morning of August 4, German troops stormed into Belgium. England hesitated no longer. She declared war on Germany at midnight.

Within a week Austria's limited war with Serbia had drawn the major powers of Europe into a bloody whirlpool. The Central Powers, Germany and Austria-Hungary, never did manage to persuade anyone that their cause was just, and they were joined only by Bulgaria and Turkey. The Allies ultimately included England, France, Russia, Italy, Belgium, Portugal, Serbia, Montenegro, Rumania, Greece, Japan, and the United States.

Ancient hatreds, unfilled ambitions, tangled alliances, and the lust for power and possessions had left a trail of tinder across the European continent. The spark from Princip's gun had ignited the tinder. A fortune teller had once predicted that Franz Ferdinand "would one day let loose a world war." The prophesy had come true.

10 · In Prison

While Austria was setting her course for war, the authorities in Sarajevo and elsewhere were busy trying to round up everyone associated with the plot against Franz Ferdinand. The first assassin to be arrested was Nedeljko Čabrinović, who had thrown the bomb at the Archduke. He had swallowed his poison and leaped into the river, but he was dragged out alive and beaten by bystanders. When he was led into the town hall for questioning, he was bleeding from the blows. The poison had burned his mouth and throat but it did not kill him.

Leo Pfeffer, an investigations judge of the Sarajevo district court, was appointed to question Čabrinović. Before he could begin, a second assassin was dragged in, bleeding and vomiting. It was Gavrilo Princip. After firing the fatal shots he had put his pistol to his head to kill himself, but someone seized his hand. As the crowd started to beat him, he was able to slip the poison into his mouth, but it failed him just as it had failed Čabrinović. No one knows exactly why. The youths believed that they had been given cyanide. If this were true, the cyanide apparently had been weakened by exposure to air. It is also possible that they received a less deadly poison and did not take a large enough dose.

Pfeffer described Princip as "undersized, emaciated, sallow, sharp-featured. It was difficult to imagine that so frail-looking an individual could have committed so serious a deed. Even his clear blue eyes, burning and piercing but serene, had nothing cruel or criminal in their expression."

Later in the day, Princip was formally charged with the murder of Franz Ferdinand and Sophie Chotek. He replied, "I acknowledge it and do not complain, but I am sorry that I have killed the Duchess . . . because I had no intention of killing her."

The assassins had agreed that whoever succeeded would kill himself so he could not be tortured into revealing the names of the other conspirators. But when their suicides failed, both Princip and Čabrinović realized that they had never decided what to tell the authorities if they were captured alive.

Both youths tried to protect each other and all their accomplices. But under questioning they began to reveal details that made it possible for the police to begin searching for other suspects. Princip was asked where he lived, and when he gave Ilić's address, the schoolteacher was arrested. In Ilić's pocket the police found the paper-wrapped poison he had forgotten to give to Grabež.

The police also jailed some of Čabrinović's relatives

and the family's servants. From them they learned that Čabrinović had said he had come from Belgrade with two other youths. Since they already had Princip, the police began to look for the third accomplice. Grabež aroused suspicion by trying illegally to cross into Serbia. When the police found that his identification card, which Čabrinović had used, showed that he had crossed into Bosnia on May 30, they sent him back to Sarajevo for questioning.

The police now had three assassins and Ilić in custody. They tortured Grabež but he refused to confess. On July 2, Princip asked if he could see Ilić and Grabež. By this time he knew that innocent Serbs had been arrested because of the assassination and that innocent peasants were being hanged. The three conspirators were brought together that afternoon. To Grabež Princip said, "Confess everything . . . so that just people do not come to harm." To Ilić he said, "Since the court has already learned much, and so that we can save the innocent, it is necessary that you tell everything—among whom you divided the weapons and where the weapons are."

Princip meant that Ilić, who had organized the plot in Sarajevo, should reveal the names of the other three assassins. But once Ilić started talking, he did not stop. He not only gave the authorities the names of the other assassins but enough additional information to implicate the Black Hand agents and the peasants who had helped Princip and Grabež cross the border.

Pfeffer, the investigating judge, later claimed that Ilić had talked in the hope that his life would be spared.

The other three assassins had fled Sarajevo, but now the police knew whom they were looking for. Vaso Čubrilović was arrested in western Bosnia on July 3. Popović later described in detail what he did from the moment Čabrinović's bomb exploded until the moment he too was caught.

"The crowd started to run and the police whistled and women were heard screaming from all sides. I was immediately conscious of the danger I was in. . . . A thought came into my mind as fast as lightning: Get rid of the weapons as soon as possible. I ran along Čumurija Street, entered the first courtyard, and left the weapons and potassium cyanide in a cellar. When I returned to the river promenade . . . I heard someone saying that nothing had happened . . . while others claimed that the heir apparent was lightly wounded. As the secret policemen were still arresting anyone on the river promenade who looked suspicious, I went to the Corso. People on the Corso still did not know anything.

"After a short time a clamor began in the upper part of the Corso. . . . I pushed my way through in order to see what was the matter. Some were saying that three bombs had exploded, others said that two persons had shot out of pistols—almost

every man was saying something different. . . .
Still . . . I learned that . . . there had been an
attempt to kill [Franz Ferdinand] with a revolver
on his way back from the town hall. Only nobody
knew the outcome of this attentat. As the heir apparent had interrupted his festive passage along the
streets and returned to the konak, I came to the
conclusion that something must have happened to
someone. I ran back to the place where I had left
the weapons, but I found the doors of the courtyard
shut. Then I went home and burned everything
that could have served as a reason for my arrest, because I knew that searches and arrests would start
everywhere.

"I again returned to the river promenade. On
the way there I heard several times that the bomb
was thrown by a worker, Čabrinović. I thought
that people mispronounced the name of Vaso Čubrilović and was certain that he had thrown the bomb.
But again I could not hear anything of the heir
apparent's condition.

"After lunch I set off to [see] Kranjčević in order
to hear what Vaso had done. Just as I was crossing
the bridge . . . a big black banner was lowered
from the roof of the new post office! Someone had
paid with his head and it must have been one of the
bigwigs if they were running up black flags on government offices. I felt a weight off my soul. I
cheerfully hastened to Kranjčević. I saw a woman

131

who was crying aloud and when she was asked by a German why she was crying, she answered, 'Both are dead.'

"Thus we had succeeded. In fact I didn't know who 'both' were, but 'he' was certainly included, because a German woman would not cry for just anybody openly in the street.

"I learned from Kranjčević that the bomb was not thrown by Vaso, but by the typographer, Čabrinović, and that Princip had fired on the return trip from the town hall. Several persons had been wounded by the bomb and the heir apparent and his wife were dead. Princip had mortally wounded them both.

"After that I became completely listless. Our action had succeeded and now they could impale us. Almost insolently I stared into every passerby's face in order to see if the act had made an impression on him. Once more I went for my weapons but the gate was still locked. . . .

"On Tuesday I set off home to Zemun [where his family lived]. As I did not have a regular school identity card, a police patrol took me off the train at Zenica and not until Saturday was I able to continue my journey. I arrived in Zemun at 6 o'clock on Sunday. . . .

"As soon as I arrived home, I gave my father the permit I had been given by the police in Zenica to take to the town hall and report my arrival. He was told there that I personally must come. I had a presentiment of approaching danger and thought of escaping. Still, I thought that if they had some news which would induce them to arrest me, they would not send word through my father to call on them, but would immediately send a patrol. . . . I had read in [a newspaper] the list of persons who had been arrested in connection with the assassination and except for Danilo Ilić, nobody knew anything about me. As for Ilić, I was certain that he would not utter a word. Therefore I decided to go.

"When I arrived at the police station I was told . . . that I was to be arrested and taken to Sarajevo at once because of my participation in the assassination. . . . The clerk who was to interrogate me either was a good nationalist or was convinced that I was not guilty and instead of questioning me . . . he immediately read me everything they had communicated from Sarajevo. Everything he read to me was true and that indicated that Ilić had told everything. Therefore, when the clerk asked me what I had to say in my defense, I answered: 'Everything is true.' He was dumbfounded. He could not believe that there stood in front of him one of the assassins of the late heir apparent.

"I was brought to Sarajevo on Tuesday, July 7. I was ordered to stand in front of a wall in the police courtyard and to look at one spot with the re-

133

mark that if I glanced in any other direction they would beat me like a dog. A soldier with a bayonet on his rifle walked behind me. Thus I stood for an hour and then an officer came with two soldiers and drove me to the military prison in a carriage. They locked me up into the first cell on the second floor. After the jailer had told me the regulations, he pointed to a board built into the wall. A number of iron rings were fastened to it as well as to the floor beneath it. 'Here we shall hang you by your thumbs if you don't tell everything!' he said. When I was left alone, I started to look at that board with horror and I imagined the worst tortures, although it was not clear to me how one is hung 'by his thumbs.' "

But Popović was never hung by his thumbs or tortured in any way. "I was lucky," he later said. "By the time they arrested me they had all the information they needed." However, he did have a difficult time explaining to the police why one bullet was missing from his revolver when they recovered it. They thought he had also fired at the Archduke, but the missing bullet was the one Ilić had fired into the tunnel wall.

The only assassin who succeeded in escaping was Mehmed Mehmedbašić. On June 30, two days after the murder, he left Sarajevo by train and returned to Hercegovina. From there he fled into Montenegro.

In Montenegro, the assassins were honored as heroes, and Mehmedbašić could not resist the temptation to boast that he was one of them. He was arrested by the Montenegrin police, and Austria demanded that he be returned for trial.

But Montenegro had little love for Austria. Mehmedbašić was quietly permitted to escape from prison, while the Montenegrins assured the angry Austrians that they would be happy to turn him over if only they could find him. Mehmedbašić hid in Montenegro until November, when he crossed into Serbia to fight with the Serbians in World War I.

Even after war was declared, Austrian authorities were still rounding up suspects. Among those arrested were a number of Young Bosnians; some of the peasants who had helped two of the assassins cross the border; Veljko Čubrilović, the schoolteacher who had aided them in Priboj; and Mihajlo Jovanović, the wealthy businessman who had hidden the weapons under his dining table.

The suspects were locked in separate cells in the military prison in Sarajevo, and all of them were put in chains. In his solitude, Popović remembered a book he had read which described how imprisoned Russian revolutionaries communicated by knocking on the walls of their cells. Popović decided to try it. He wrote the alphabet, with a number under each letter, and the word *knock* on the inside of the lid of a water pail. Since water pails and metal plates were circulated among the prisoners three times a day, Popović wrote his code on every pail and plate that came into his hands. In ten days the prisoners had organized their communications system. Eventually they perfected it so well that within two hours a message could circulate through the cells on all three floors of the prison. Popović was even able to use the system of knocks to play chess and other games with his fellow prisoners.

One morning, when Popović got the prison garbage can in his cell, he found a note inside which said that the European war had begun. Popović immediately communicated this news to the others, who were elated. "We felt that the fate of our ideas was being solved," he later wrote. The conspirators hoped that the war would destroy Austria-Hungary and give Bosnia the gift of liberty.

From other prisoners Popović heard news of the war, which he wanted to pass on to his companions. He decided to start a newspaper. With a nail, he drew a rectangle on the bottom of his metal plate. At the top of the rectangle he scratched in the name of the newspaper, *The Messtin*. Under it he wrote the subtitle, "The Newspaper of the Revengers." Then, in very professional style, he scratched in the number of the newspaper and the date. *The Messtin* published both war and prison news, and on Saturday there was a humor column written by another pris-

136

oner. There were three different editions of the paper daily, or one after each meal.

The idea caught on, and several of the other prisoners founded their own newspapers. All were on metal plates and all circulated each time the guards served the meals. The news columns were generally devoted to attacks on Austria, poetry, and a certain grim prison humor. Once the rumor spread that Ilić had hanged himself in his cell. Several of the editors were composing special memorial editions when Princip's plate came by with "News from the Other World." "Charon did not want to take Danilo Ilić across the river Styx," reported Princip, "because he had too much work with the sinful Ferdinand. Ilić is alive and sends his greetings."

On September 28, with a great clanking of chains, the prisoners were taken from their cells and brought together to hear the indictment read to them. They stared at each other, amused and amazed. Some of the conspirators had never even met. All of them looked grotesque, because for three months they had been unable to shave, get haircuts, or change their clothes. Being young and highspirited, the boys just laughed at each other.

No one bothered to listen to Judge Pfeffer as he read the charges against them. They were too busy exchanging greetings. Finally the judge scolded them

137

for behaving like children when their lives were at stake. "You must understand us, sir," replied Princip. "We see one another for the first time after such a long period. What you are reading to us we already know, and we know our fate."

After reading the indictment, the judge said the prisoners could raise objections to it if they wished, although this might delay the trial. "I want to raise an objection," said Čabrinović. "Outside there is a war, and nobody knows what will happen tomorrow." The judge understood what Čabrinović was thinking. "You do not hope to be liberated?" he asked. "We would sooner hang fourteen Čabrinovićes than let you go free!" Boldly Čabrinović retorted, "Those who would hang us should beware." But urged by the others, who wanted to be tried as soon as possible, he withdrew his objection.

On October 11 the assassins and their accomplices were given shaves and haircuts, and the chains were removed from their ankles. The following day, their trial began.

11 · On Trial

O n October 12, 1914, in a large room of the military barracks in Sarajevo, twenty-five persons
were brought to trial in connection with the murder of
Franz Ferdinand. Thus the trial began ten weeks after Austria had used the defendants' guilt as an excuse
to start World War I.

Twenty-two of the defendants were charged with
murder and high treason. They included the five
assassins who had been caught and some of their accomplices: Danilo Ilić, who had plotted the murder in
Sarajevo; Veljko Čubrilović, the schoolteacher who
had helped two of the youths in Priboj; and Mihajlo
Jovanović, the businessman who had hidden the
weapons under his dining table. Also charged with
murder and treason were eight of the peasants who
had helped the two youths cross the border and six
Young Bosnians, including Popović's friend Ivo Kranjčević. The three remaining defendants were relatives of Kranjčević, two men and a woman, in whose
house Kranjčević had hidden Vaso Čubrilović's weapons after the assassination. They were charged with
complicity in the crime.

The penalty for murder and treason was death. However, under Austrian law, no one could be executed if he was less than twenty years of age at the time of his crime. Not one of the five assassins on trial had been twenty on June 28.

The trial was conducted according to Austrian law. Thus those who were guilty were treated more fairly than the innocent Bosnian peasants who were hanged without any trial at all. Three judges conducted the trial and, since there was no jury, they would decide on the defendants' guilt as well as pass sentences. As is common in European trials, the judges, not the prosecutor, asked most of the questions. But there was a prosecutor, the attorney general of Sarajevo, whose son had walked with Princip on the morning of the murder. The defendants had court-appointed attorneys. Six journalists were present and the public was admitted by invitation.

On the first day of the trial, the prosecutor read the indictment. Then everyone was returned to his cell except Čabrinović, who was questioned by the presiding judge, Luigi von Curinaldi. After Čabrinović, it was Princip's turn, and then came the other defendants, one by one. After each was questioned he was permitted to remain in the courtroom for the rest of the trial.

Curinaldi asked each of the defendants if he pleaded guilty. None of the assassins denied his part in the plot, although Princip denied that he felt guilty.

140

"I am not a criminal," he said, "for I have removed an evildoer. I meant to do a good deed." Princip emphasized that he intended to kill Franz Ferdinand but not the Duchess. At one point during the proceedings the judge read aloud Count Harrach's account of the assassination, which included the Archduke's dying plea to his wife, "Live for our children."

All the defendants lowered their heads, and Princip closed his eyes. Later, one of the attorneys asked Princip if the reading had affected him. Angrily Princip replied, "Do you think I am an animal and have no feelings?"

Although they regretted Sophie's accidental death, the assassins felt no remorse for Franz Ferdinand. They justified their deed by the ancient law of tyrannicide. One of the Young Bosnians was asked, "Therefore, you are of the opinion that there are cases when assassination is necessary?"

"Yes, there are."

"In which cases?"

"When the man is a tyrant."

Grabež expressed the same feeling a little differently. He said, "When we heard that Franz Ferdinand was coming here, and knowing all the evils that our nation had suffered from him and from Austria, we decided to pay Austria back through the heir apparent."

Popović told the judge that the assassination was a symbolic rather than an actual act of tyrannicide.

The assassins were not as interested in the specific victim as they were in avenging "the persecution of our people." Asked by the judge to describe this persecution, the youths, in their turn, listed the Austrian abuses against the empire's Slavs and the refusal of the monarchy to grant the Slavs the right of self-rule. All of the assassins said they wanted to see the Austrian empire destroyed and the South Slavs freed. Čabrinović commented, "A state which . . . subjugates other states could not be regarded as stable. . . . Its whole strength lies in bayonets."

Princip was particularly bitter because the Austrians had done nothing about land reform in Bosnia and Hercegovina. "The people have been impoverished; they are treated like cattle," he said. "I am the son of a serf, and I know what life is like in the villages."

The judge asked the assassins to describe their political beliefs. Popović replied that he was "a champion of the unity of Serbs, Croats, and Slovenes" in a South Slav state. The other youths, in different words, supported this view. Princip said, "I am a South Slav nationalist, aiming for the unification of all South Slavs."

"A unification under Austria?" asked Curinaldi.

"God save us from that!" replied Princip.

Though all of the assassins reeled off political and moral reasons to justify their act, it was the emotional Čabrinović who revealed the highly personal motives that may shape an assassin. During the trial the judge read a letter from Čabrinović's tyrannical father, in which the old man complained about his ungrateful children. Čabrinović commented, "I do not wish to denounce my own father, but if his teaching had been better, I would not be sitting on this bench."

The older defendants were not as bold or outspoken as the younger ones. The schoolteacher Veljko Čubrilović of Priboj and the merchant Mihajlo Jovanović of Tuzla admitted helping Princip and Grabež, but said they did not believe in terror as a political weapon and did not support a revolution against Austria. Danilo Ilić testified that he had first agreed to the assassination and then tried to stop it.

The peasants hardly knew what to say in their defense. Asked if he was guilty, one of them replied, weeping, "It is possible that I am a little guilty." Later, when the same man was asked why he did not tell the police about the weapons he had seen, he answered, "But with us one cannot do a thing like that without the permission of the head of the family."

After the initial questioning of the defendants, the prosecutor read aloud various revolutionary pamphlets and articles to illustrate what the assassins believed in. One called for an insurrection against Austria. Curinaldi asked Princip if he agreed with this and Princip replied, "Not only do I agree with this, but if I could I would destroy the whole Austro-Hungarian monarchy!" After that, when the judge asked the

143

youths for their opinions of the articles he skipped Princip with the wry remark, "We already know what you think."

The chief reason for reading this material to the court was to prove that the assassins had been influenced by Serbian propaganda. The prosecutor had to insist that the crime had originated in Serbia, since Austria had plunged the world into war on that claim, but he was unable to offer any proof and the youths repeatedly denied the charge. The three assassins who had come from Belgrade pointed out that they had to be cautious to avoid detection by Serbian authorities. Grabež said simply, "I was led not by Serbia but solely by Bosnia." Princip said, "Serbia had nothing to do with it, and so cannot be responsible for our deed."

The prosecutor also raised the question of Princip's age. According to the parish register in his village, Princip was born on July 13, 1894. According to the civil register, he was born on June 13. That month meant a matter of life or death for Princip, for if he were twenty on the day of the assassination, he was old enough to hang.

Almost an entire day was spent arguing this issue. Princip's mother said her son was born in July, not June. This was confirmed by the village priest who had made the entry in both records. He said he had made an error in recording the date in the civil register because it had been done from illegible notes weeks after the boy was born. The judges announced they would consider the evidence and reveal their decision when they presented their verdict.

When it was time for the defense, the attorneys found themselves in a difficult position. They did not dare attempt to justify the assassination, so they blamed their clients' acts on Serbian propaganda or on the other defendants. After Čabrinović's lawyer attacked the ideals of Young Bosnia, Čabrinović rose and said it would have been better if his attorney had not spoken for him, for his accusations were worse than the prosecutor's.

Only one lawyer took his duties seriously. He was a socialist, Dr. Rudolf Cistler, who defended four of the accused. First he delivered a review of the development of nationalism since the French Revolution. Judge Curinaldi told him he was being long-winded. Then Dr. Cistler startled the court with an astonishing argument. Some of the defendants may have been guilty of murder, he said, but none could be guilty of treason. No one could be accused of treason for trying to free Bosnia and Hercegovina because they were not legally part of the empire.

Austria had occupied the two provinces in 1878. Two years later, the Austrian parliament passed a law stating that there could be no change in the territorial status of the provinces without the consent of the parliaments of both Austria and Hungary. In 1908, Austria-Hungary annexed Bosnia and Herce-

govina. Bills legalizing the annexation had been sub-
mitted to both parliaments, but neither one had gotten
around to approving them. It was therefore true that
according to the Austrian law of 1880, the two provinces had not been legally made part of the empire,
and the defendants could not be charged with treason.

Judge Curinaldi was so shocked by this argument
that he suppressed it. He reprimanded Dr. Cistler and
told him that if he continued in this manner he would
be forbidden to speak. After the trial, Dr. Cistler was
banished from Sarajevo.

The trial ended on October 23, barely two weeks
after it began. Čabrinović made a last rambling
statement both justifying and apologizing for the
crime and appealing to the Archduke's children to for-
give him. Princip's final statement was terse. "As far
as suggestions are concerned that somebody talked us
into committing the assassination, that is not true," he
said. "The idea for the assassination grew among us,
and we realized it. We loved our people. In my own
defense I have nothing to say."

Five days later, the judges delivered the verdicts
and the sentences. They decided the conflicting evidence on Princip's birthdate in his favor; he had not
been twenty on the day of the assassination. Therefore, Princip, Čabrinović, and Grabež, the three
youths who had come from Belgrade, received the
maximum sentence their age would allow—twenty

146

years at hard labor. Once a month they would have to fast, and each year, on the anniversary of the murder, they would be put in a darkened cell for twenty-four hours.

The two students from Sarajevo, Vaso Čubrilović and Cvetko Popović, were sentenced to thirteen years. But Čubrilović received an additional three years because he had offended the presiding judge in the course of the trial. Curinaldi had commented that if Čubrilović believed in God, as he insisted he did, he would not commit murder. Čubrilović replied, "And who murders millions of men in European wars?"

"You are to blame for all that," said the judge.

"Not I, but people like the heir apparent," replied the defiant Čubrilović.

Four of the six Young Bosnians got prison terms ranging from three to ten years. Two others were acquitted. The three relatives of Ivo Kranjčević who were charged with complicity in the crime were also acquitted.

Of the eight peasants, four were acquitted, two received prison terms, and two were sentenced to hang. One was the man who did not go to the police because he needed permission of the head of the family.

Three other men were sentenced to hang. They were Danilo Ilić, who had organized the plot in Sarajevo; Veljko Čubrilović, who had helped the youths in Priboj; and Mihajlo Jovanović, who had hidden the weapons under his dining table.

12 · "We Loved Our People"

The sentences were reviewed by a higher court, which made only two changes. The death sentences of the two peasants were changed to prison terms. The other three men were hanged in Sarajevo on February 3, 1915.

Veljko Čubrilović, the Priboj schoolteacher, was first. He had difficulty loosening his tie and collar to make way for the noose, but he refused the hangman's offer of assistance. Mihajlo Jovanović, the Tuzla merchant, was second, and Danilo Ilić was last. Drums beat throughout the executions so the priest could barely hear their last words, but he said, "All three went to their death with dignity, acclaiming fatherland and freedom." Greater praise came from the hangman himself, who reported, "As an Austrian loyal to my own sovereign, I can assure you that I never met such brave, calm delinquents in all my experience."

Because the Austrians feared that the three men would become martyrs, like Bogdan Žerajić, they buried them secretly, outside of Sarajevo. But a boy from a nearby village saw the Sarajevo police dig the three graves on the night of the hanging. He told his elders, and after the war, the bodies were found and returned to Sarajevo.

Even after the Sarajevo conspirators had been tried and executed or imprisoned, the Austrians continued their massive retaliation against Serbs throughout Bosnia and Hercegovina. Young Bosnians were arrested in every town in the two provinces. Many were tried and sentenced to prison and even death, but executions were unnecessary. The Austrians wiped out a whole generation of rebels by putting the youths in the army and sending them to the front as cannon fodder.

The older Serbs were imprisoned in concentration camps by the tens of thousands. Most died of disease and malnutrition. Disease and malnutrition also took their toll of the conspirators. Of the thirteen sentenced to prison, only five survived.

Ten of the conspirators were sent to Zenica, the largest prison in the provinces, although they were later transferred to other prisons. Princip, Čabrinović, and Grabež were imprisoned at Theresienstadt, in the northern part of the empire. They were not tortured, but prison life was torture enough. Each wore chains weighing over twenty pounds. The food was bad and there was little of it. The cells were dark and cold, and since the youths were kept in solitary confinement, the loneliness was maddening.

Princip had tuberculosis even before he was imprisoned; Čabrinović and Grabež may also have had the disease. Prison conditions nurtured their illness. Before the end of 1915, Čabrinović was transferred to a hospital, but since his condition was incurable, he was ordered back to prison. He died of tuberculosis on January 23, 1916, at the age of twenty-one.

The second youth, Grabež, died during the winter of 1916 of chronic starvation. He too was twenty-one.

Gavrilo Princip died more slowly. In the nightmare of his Austrian prison, tuberculosis devoured his body. By the beginning of 1916 his flesh and bones had begun to rot with the disease, and he had running sores on his chest and arms. He tried to hang himself with a towel but failed. In April, 1916, he was transferred to the hospital at Theresienstadt, and he spent the next two years going back and forth between the hospital and his cell.

A psychiatrist left a record of Princip's thoughts and his agony. The youth described the horrors of solitary confinement and how he suffered most from not having anything to read. He also told the doctor that he did not feel responsible for World War I because it would have come anyway, and that he hoped all the South Slavs would unite in a republic. Ivo Kranjčević, who saw Princip at Theresienstadt, wrote that Princip told him he did not expect to live to the end of the war but that "the end of Austria was certain, and that he had opened the road to her doom."

Tuberculosis continued to gnaw at Princip's frail body, destroying his left elbow. Doctors had to connect the lower part of his arm to the upper part with a silver wire. Finally, the arm was amputated. One doctor wrote of the dying Princip, "the eyes, sunken in their sockets, had lost their brightness and the fire of youth. Except when he was speaking about the liberation of his people, then they would brighten up for a moment."

When he was still able to do so, Princip used a nail to scratch some poetry on the walls of his cell and on his drinking mug. One verse read, "The time drags on slowly and there is nothing new. Today everything is as it was yesterday and will be so tomorrow. But Žerajić was right to say: 'He who wants to live, let him die. He who wants to die, let him live.'"

Gavrilo Princip died of tuberculosis of the bone on April 28, 1918, in the hospital at Theresienstadt. He was twenty-three years old.

The Austrians, still skittish about providing the Serbs with more martyrs, buried him secretly in the local Roman Catholic cemetery. The grave was dug in the middle of a path and the ground was leveled so no one would know a body lay there. But the Austrians' tragedy, in matters large and small, was that they never could understand how much they were

151

hated by the people they ruled. One of the soldiers in the burial detail was a Czech. That same night he made a map of the cemetery, showing the location of Princip's grave. After the war he returned to the cemetery and put a Czech flag over the grave. In 1920, Princip's bones were reburied in Sarajevo.

Three of the other five conspirators who died in prison were peasants and two were Young Bosnians. The youngest to be sentenced, Marko Perin, died before the end of 1914 at the age of seventeen. Of the five who survived, one was a peasant and four were Young Bosnians, including the two assassins recruited from among the students of Sarajevo, Vaso Čubrilović and Cvetko Popović.

The survivors were freed when the war ended in November, 1918. The Austro-Hungarian empire had been shattered. The assassins had snapped the wire, and the broken pot lay in shards.

The war was fought on many fronts, but the conspirators, in their cells, cared only for the fate of Serbia. An Austrian army commanded by General Oskar Potiorek attacked Serbia in August, 1914. Within two weeks the Serbians had thrown Potiorek's men back to the border and were crossing into Austrian territory. The captive soldiers of Austria's army were no match for the Serbians; they fought for a cause they did not support, while the Serbians fought for survival.

Potiorek attacked again in September and captured Belgrade in December, but the Serbians recaptured it two weeks later, and Potiorek was relieved of his command. Since the Austrians were also being battered by the Russians, the war in Serbia virtually ceased during the early months of 1915, while Germany came to Austria's rescue on the Russian front. But while war rested, its closest ally, disease, was active. Over 150,000 of the weak, the homeless, and the hungry died of typhus and other plagues.

After the Germans had driven the Russians back, they turned to the Balkans. In October, 1915, Germany and Austria attacked Serbia in the north while Bulgaria marched into Macedonia. Serbia was to be crushed between her three enemies. Belgrade fell on October 9, and the Serbian army began to retreat toward Kosovo Polje, where Prince Lazar had made his stand over five centuries earlier.

The aged King Petar of Serbia was too ill to walk and had to be carried. His son, Prince Regent Alexandar, had to have his appendix removed in a cottage along the way, and then he too was carried. Behind the retreating army came monks bearing the bodies of the kings who had made Serbia great during the Middle Ages, along with other sacred objects. Thus, carrying their kings both living and dead, the Serbians came to Kosovo, once before the grave of their freedom.

There a decision had to be made. The Serbians were surrounded; the only opening was in the south-west. They could surrender, they could die at Kosovo, or they could retreat through Montenegro and Albania to the Adriatic coast and return, with Allied help, to fight another day. The Serbians rejected the first two alternatives. They would neither surrender nor would they water the fields of Kosovo with their blood a second time. Instead they chose temporary retreat. As the first snows of winter drifted down, the Serbians turned toward the rugged mountains at their backs.

Some 250,000 men started up the 5,000-foot peaks, along with 35,000 youths who would be old enough to fight when the army returned. Many never came down again. They were assaulted by cold, hunger, and disease, and the men ate dead horses, boots, and the bark of trees. Now that they were in retreat they were cannibalized by their neighbors, for small nations are no kinder to each other than large ones. Montenegro, Albania, Italy, and Greece saw in Serbia's defeat an opportunity to promote their own interests in the Balkans. The Greeks refused to let Allied armies in Salonika come to Serbia's rescue. The King of Montenegro, safely in Paris, ordered his countrymen to refuse food to the starving Serbians. Armed Albanian snipers shot at the numbed soldiers as they struggled through the mountains. When they finally reached the Adriatic coast, the Italians refused to send ships to rescue them.

Before the Serbian army was finally evacuated to

the French-held island of Corfu, 100,000 soldiers and 20,000 youths died.   Yet the survivors returned to the mainland in the summer of 1916 and in November they recaptured 400 square miles of Macedonia from the Bulgarians.   They were back on Serbian soil, and they were never again driven off.

During the bleakest years of the war, there was a strange postscript to the Sarajevo assassination.   Serbia's defeats had aggravated the conflict between the civil and military authorities over who would rule. Prince Alexandar of Serbia decided that he had to destroy Colonel Apis before Apis destroyed him.   The Prince also knew that Austria, in secretly negotiating with the Allies for peace, had demanded that everyone connected with the Sarajevo assassination be punished, and that all anti-Austrian societies in Serbia be dissolved.

Alexandar saw a chance to rid himself of his greatest enemy, satisfy the Austrians, and demonstrate that the Serbian government was innocent of involvement in the Sarajevo conspiracy.   In December, 1916, Apis and other Black Hand leaders were arrested.   They were charged with planning to assassinate Prince Alexandar and Nikola Pašić in order to make a separate peace with Germany.   No one has yet discovered evidence to support this charge; it was apparently invented solely as a means of eliminating a dangerous rival.

Apis' trial was held at Salonika, Greece, in April, 1917. One of the defendants was Mehmed Mehmedbašić, the only Sarajevo assassin who had managed to escape. In 1916, Mehmedbašić, surely one of the most inept assassins in history, had been involved in still another plot, this time against the King of Greece. He was supposed to kill the King in a theater, but His Majesty had a cold and stayed home that day. But Mehmedbašić was not on trial for that attempt; he was accused of being part of the conspiracy against Alexandar. He denied this, saying that he could not have taken part in a plot that did not exist.

In the course of the trial, Apis was advised by one of Alexandar's men that it would be to his advantage to admit that he was responsible for the assassination of Franz Ferdinand. In a written statement to the court, Apis said he had organized the entire plot, with Russian support. This confession, whether true or not, did not save his life. He was executed by a firing squad in June for the alleged attempt to kill Alexandar. Mehmedbašić was sentenced to fifteen years in prison.

World War I ended seventeen months later, and Franz Ferdinand's prophesy was realized. The emperors of Russia and Austria had pushed each other off their thrones. Russia fought with the Allies; the Allies won but the Tsar lost. In 1917 Russia was the scene of the world's first Communist revolution, and Tsar Nicholas was sent to exile and to death.

The German monarchy also perished, and Kaiser Wilhelm was forced into exile. Though Germany was to rise again, under an Austrian named Adolf Hitler, the Habsburg dynasty fell with scarcely a whimper. Franz Josef died in November, 1916, at the age of eighty-six. His grandnephew, Karl Franz, reigned for two years before he was forced into exile and a republic was proclaimed.

In the closing days of the war, the unhappy marriage of Austria and Hungary ended, and they became two separate nations. The provinces they had ruled were eventually divided among Poland, Rumania, Italy, Czechoslovakia, and a nation called the Kingdom of Serbs, Croats, and Slovenes. It consisted of Serbia, Montenegro, and the empire's South Slav provinces: Croatia, Dalmatia, Slovenia, Bosnia, and Hercegovina. In 1929 the name of the new nation was changed to Yugoslavia, the land of the South Slavs.

Three of the six assassins lived to see their dream come true. One was the hapless Mehmedbašić, who was pardoned in 1919. He returned home to Stolac in Hercegovina, where he worked as a gardener and carpenter. During World War II he was imprisoned by the Germans and he died in 1942.

The other two survivors were the Sarajevo students, Vaso Čubrilović and Cvetko Popović. Both returned to school and chose teaching careers. For a time, Čubrilović served as an official of the Yugoslav government, but he is now a professor of history at the

157

University of Belgrade.   Popović gave up his teaching career after World War II and became a curator of ethnology at the national museum in Sarajevo, the museum that Franz Ferdinand was to have visited on the day of his death.   In 1964, Popović retired and began to write two books about the assassination.

Assassinations have always had a morbid fascination.   They deal not only with the mystery of death and the mystery of conspiracy but also with the mystery of what might have been.   If Franz Ferdinand had not been shot, would there have been a war? With the world so primed for it, could war have been averted?

Because the assassination had such awesome consequences, many have refused to accept it as the almost accidental work of a group of bumbling young patriots.   Thousands of books and articles have been written on the subject, to blame someone more convincing, or argue a special cause, or air an exotic theory.   Some hold Serbia responsible because there is evidence, which was unknown to Austria at the time, that in June, 1914, Pašić received a report that armed youths had crossed the border.   But the report did not say who they were or what their purpose was.   Nonetheless, Pašić ordered an investigation of the incident, ordered an investigation of Colonel Apis, tightened the rules preventing men and arms from crossing the border illegally, and tried to find and stop the youths.

There is also evidence that he warned Austria, but that this warning, like all the others, was shrugged off.

Some accept Apis' confession and hold him wholly to blame. Others argue that since he was chief of Serbian military intelligence, he was in league with the Serbian government, the Russian government, the Russian revolutionaries, the Germans, or the Hungarians, depending on which axe the author is grinding.

Still others say that Franz Ferdinand's many enemies in Austria planned the murder, and that the poor security arrangements and the bad judgments of June 28 were deliberate.

There are other theories as well. The Freemasons have been accused of plotting the murder, while Adolf Hitler claimed that Princip was a Jew. Princip has also been described as an illegitimate child of royalty, seeking vengeance against Franz Ferdinand. And, of course, there is one theory that Princip did not actually fire the shots; somebody else did.

The special pleaders have made their points, but none has proved his case. History often has no logic; the most complex events often have the most simple explanations. Franz Ferdinand was shot primarily because a group of young Bosnian patriots wanted their country to be free. The world was indifferent to their problem, so they set about solving it in their own primitive way. Once they succeeded, it was no longer their problem, but the world's.

Epilogue

Half a century after the assassination of Franz Ferdinand, Sarajevo is still the capital of Bosnia. But today Bosnia and Hercegovina together are one of the six republics that make up the land called Yugoslavia, and Sarajevo is the nation's third-largest city. It rests in a bed of green mountains, on a site that was inhabited before Christ was born. In the fifteenth century, under Turkish rule, Sarajevo became an important military and administrative center. The newer sections of Sarajevo are unmistakably Western, but the old part of the city still has a Turkish flavor. The domed mosques, the soaring minarets, the men in fezes and the women in ballooning trousers give Sarajevo the appearance of a land misplaced by the Near East.

The Austrians, who ruled from Sarajevo for a far briefer period than the Turks, also left their architectural mark. But while the graceful Turkish structures seem to flow from their environment, the Austrian buildings are imposed upon it. Massive in design, clumsy in detail, swollen with self-importance, they attempt to subdue the land, as the Austrians attempted to subdue the people, by sheer weight.

Retracing Franz Ferdinand's route through Sarajevo is primarily a pilgrimage from one stolid Austrian structure to another. At Ilidže, he and his wife stayed at the Hotel Bosna, which was redecorated and refurnished for their visit at great expense. Contrary to what the guidebooks say, the Hotel Bosna is not the building called the Hotel Srbija. It is a somewhat larger structure just behind the Hotel Srbija. Running vertically down one side of the building, which is now used as an orthopedic hospital, are the words *Vila Bosna*. But across the faded yellow stucco it is still possible to make out the words *Hotel Bosna* in the Cyrillic alphabet used by the Serbs.

A quay still runs along the right bank of the Miljačka River, whose waters are colored red or brownish-red by the clay of the surrounding mountains. The name of the river has not changed, but the Appel Quay is now called the Vojvode Stepe Obala, in honor of a Serbian military leader.

The obala, which is the Serbian word for quay, leads directly to the town hall, where the reception for Franz Ferdinand was held. This immense six-sided building has artificial Moorish touches at the roof, windows, and balconies, a condescending gesture of the Austrians to their Moslem subjects. In a style typical of the Austrian edifices in Bosnia, it is horizon-

161

tally striped in alternating rows of orange and buff stucco. The stucco is now cracked and peeling, but the building is still being used. It is the library for the University of Sarajevo and holds over 500,000 volumes.

About one hundred yards from the town hall, on a side street just off the market place, is the house where Mrs. Stoja Ilić lived. There her son, Danilo, and her boarder, Gavrilo Princip, argued over whether or not to kill Franz Ferdinand and there the weapons were stored until the day before Vidovdan. The house, which is marked by a plaque, has been carefully preserved, and the street is now named for Ilić.

Not far away, on the opposite side of the Miljačka River, is the konak, where Franz Ferdinand was to have had lunch. It is a brownish-orange building guarded by four stone lions. Unlike the town hall it is in excellent condition because it is used by the president of Bosnia and Hercegovina for official receptions and also serves as a guest house for foreign dignitaries. In the room where Franz Ferdinand died, all that remains from 1914 is a gold floral pattern done in ornamental plaster on the ceiling.

Facing down from the town hall, the quay is intersected on the left by a series of bridges, which cross the Miljačka River. On the right side of the quay there are houses and shops running along blocks of varying sizes and shapes; some are no wider than a single building. The first bridge below the town hall was once called the Kaiser Bridge, but it is now Žerajića Most, or Žerajić's Bridge. A plaque placed there in 1964 explains that this was the bridge from which Bogdan Žerajić fired at Governor Varešanin on June 15, 1910. This was the act that set off the string of assassination attempts that ended in the death of Franz Ferdinand.

The third bridge below the town hall was the Ču-murija Bridge in 1914 but it is now called Zrinskoga Bridge. A plaque is cemented into the stone embankment about forty-five feet beyond the bridge to show where Nedeljko Čabrinović stood when he threw his bomb at the Archduke.

It is between these two bridges, at the second bridge from the town hall, that history paused for a moment in 1914 and then turned onto a new path. The bridge was then called Lateiner Bridge; it is now Principov Most, or Princip's Bridge. It was on the corner opposite this bridge that Gavrilo Princip stood when he fired. The cobblestone span seems too insignificant to bear the weight of its place in history. It is so small and narrow that only one car can cross at a time.

On the fatal corner opposite Princip's Bridge stands the same building that was there in 1914. But Franz Josef Street is now Yugoslav Army Street and in the space once occupied by Moritz Schiller's delicatessen there is a Young Bosnia and Gavrilo Princip Museum. It is just one room, for the Young Bosnians left few

163

things behind with which to memorialize them. On one side of the museum there is a long street map of Sarajevo showing where each of the assassins stood along the Archduke's route. Most of the rest of the exhibits are photographs, of the assassins, the leaders of Young Bosnia, Franz Ferdinand, Ilić's house, Princip's parents in their peasants' dress. There are also several photographs of the Serb peasants who were hanged in retaliation for Franz Ferdinand's death. One shows some Austrian soldiers posing around the corpse of a peasant swinging from the gallows. The Austrians are leaning past each other to be certain they will get into the photograph.

There is one rather bare display case in the center of the room with some personal effects of the assassins, including the white collar the schoolteacher Veljko Čubrilović had difficulty in loosening for the hangman. On the far wall of the museum there is a heroic bust of Princip with his words, "We loved our people."

The museum was built in 1953. At the same time, a pair of footsteps was set into the sidewalk outside, about twelve feet along Yugoslav Army Street, to show where Princip stood when he fired. They are purely symbolic, for Princip had been dead for thirty-five years when they were made, and experts differ on the question of his exact position.

Princip himself is now buried in the First Serbian Orthodox Cemetery of Sarajevo, not far from the site of the assassination. After World War I, the bones of Princip, nine of the other conspirators, and Bogdan Žerajić were placed in a massive concrete grave just to the right of the cemetery entrance. Then in 1939, for the twenty-fifth anniversary of the assassination, the Serbian Orthodox community of Sarajevo erected a chapel in the cemetery to serve as Princip's tomb.

Built into the front of the chapel are a red brick arch and cross, and under the arch is a slab of polished black granite with the epitaph, "Happy is he who lives forever for he has had reason to be born." Beneath the epitaph is the notation, "The Heroes of Vidovdan." Eleven names are listed but according to the caretaker only six bodies actually lie behind a plaster wall within the chapel. They are the remains of Princip, Čabrinović, Grabež, Veljko Čubrilović, Mihajlo Jovanović, and Bogdan Žerajić. The other five bodies remain in the original concrete tomb. The concrete has cracked and the grave is overgrown with weeds, but the chapel is carefully tended and a vase of flowers always stands before the names of the assassins.

Yugoslavs today do not think of Gavrilo Princip very often, but when they do it is with admiration. They do not remember him as an assassin or as the youth who may have started World War I. To them he is, like Miloš Obilić, a hero who slew a foreign tyrant, the patriot who gave his life to free them from Austria.

The citizens of Sarajevo seem largely indifferent to their city's place in history. Tourists come to the famous corner, their shoulders hunched under the weight of their cameras, to take photographs of the footsteps and of Princip's Bridge. Passersby will sometimes stare at the tourists but rarely at the footsteps. For them this corner is like any other, and the bridge is just a way of getting across the Miljačka River.

But not everyone in Sarajevo has forgotten Vidovdan of 1914. About a dozen old men still live in the city who were Young Bosnians plotting feverishly against the Austrians half a century ago. They are good friends and meet regularly, often at the house of Ivo Kranjčević, who is seriously ill *. Each year on Vidovdan they mark the hour of Franz Ferdinand's death by standing together, their heads bared and bowed, before Princip's tomb.

The most important of them is Dr. Cvetko Popović. The other surviving assassin, Vaso Čubrilović, lives in Belgrade, but Dr. Popović has chosen to make his home in Sarajevo, even though he lived elsewhere for most of his life. He is a small, gray-haired man, a father and a grandfather. Strolling down the hill from his home with a string bag dangling from his hand he looks like any other old man on his way to market. But unlike most old men, Dr. Popović bears a special burden—the burden of history.

* Kranjčević died on January 22, 1968, at the age of seventy-two.

Dr. Popović dismisses his role in the plot as minor. But as one of the survivors, he feels responsible for setting the story straight, an impossible task since the details have been clouded by so many myths, theories, and contradictions that even the most astute historians are not entirely certain where the truth lies. Besides, he cannot view the evidence impartially because he has become too deeply involved.

Dr. Popović not only lived through the assassination as a youth, but he relives it over and over again. Although he is shy and rather brusque, he gets so carried away when he retells the story that he begins to reenact it. With an embarrassed grin he stuffs his fists into his pockets to show how absurdly his jacket bulged on the morning of the assassination, and he demonstrates with a quick thrust how Čabrinović tossed the bomb underhand at the Archduke's car.

His general criticism of most books on the assassination is that the authors look for its causes in the wrong place. "They study Austrian origins and political origins, but they are not familiar with the situation in Bosnia," he said. "Anybody who doesn't know the special situation that existed in Bosnia can't understand why and how the assassination occurred.

"We were quite lost. Austria treated Bosnia like a colony. Everything was German. We wanted to destroy Franz Ferdinand, and the Austrians, and their German ideas. We were desperate. We wanted our freedom."

167

Dr. Popović absolutely denies that Serbia was involved in the plot and he scoffs at the suggestion that Apis was responsible for it. "His only role was to give us arms," he declared. "The idea came from the students." He agrees with most historians that Apis' trial at Salonika was staged and he called Apis' execution, "internal political murder."

With a perspective of more than fifty years, Dr. Popović now feels that "if we had known World War I would result, the assassination would not have happened. We didn't think anything like that would be the result; it was the sixth assassination attempt in four years. It was a local affair, a personal affair. We didn't think of the world or of any other country. It was our problem and we were solving it in our own way."

He says he does not know if there would have been a war even without the assassination. But when he was asked if he thought the assassination had triggered the war he replied with great certainty, "It was the immediate cause. World War I began here, at Princip's Bridge."

Bibliography

BOOKS RECOMMENDED FOR THOSE WHO WISH TO
PURSUE THE SUBJECT:

Crankshaw, Edward. *The Fall of the House of Habsburg*. London: Longmans, 1963.
A sympathetic history of Austria.

Dedijer, Vladimir. *The Road to Sarajevo*. New York: Simon and Schuster, 1966.
The best account of the assassination available in English.

Heppell, Muriel, and F. B. Singleton. *Yugoslavia*. New York: Praeger, 1961.
A simple, readable history of Yugoslavia.

Taylor, A. J. P. *The Habsburg Monarchy, 1809–1918*. New York: Harper Torchbooks (paper), 1965.
An unsympathetic history of Austria.

Tuchman, Barbara. *The Guns of August*. New York: Dell (paper), 1963.
A detailed account of the opening days of World War I.

West, Rebecca. *Black Lamb and Grey Falcon: A*

Journey through Yugoslavia. New York: Viking, 1941.

To be read as literature as well as history and commentary. The best book ever written, and ever likely to be written, about Yugoslavia.

IN ADDITION TO THE ABOVE, THE FOLLOWING VOLUMES WERE CONSULTED:

Albertini, Luigi. *The Origins of the War of 1914*. Vol. 2. London: Oxford University Press, 1953.

Ashley, Percy. *Europe from Waterloo to Sarajevo*. New York: Knopf, 1926.

Cambridge Medieval History. Vol. 4. Cambridge: Cambridge University Press, 1936.

Edmonds, James. *A Short History of World War I*. London: Oxford University Press, 1951.

Eisenmenger, Victor. *Archduke Francis Ferdinand*. London: Selwyn & Blount, 1931.

Evans, Arthur. *Illyrian Letters*. London: Longmans, 1878.

————. *Through Bosnia and the Herzegovina on Foot during the Insurrection*. London: Longmans, 1877.

Hoffman, George, and Frederick Neal. *Yugoslavia and the New Communism*. New York: Twentieth Century Fund, 1962.

Jászi, Oszkár, and John D. Lewis. *Against the Tyrant: The Tradition and Theory of Tyrannicide*. Glencoe, Ill.: The Free Press, 1957.

Kerner, Robert J., ed. *Yugoslavia*. Berkeley: University of California Press, 1949.

Locke, John. *Two Treatises of Government*. Cambridge: Cambridge University Press, 1960.

Marriott, J. A. R. *The Eastern Question.* London: Oxford University Press, 1940.

Pauli, Hertha. *The Secret of Sarajevo.* New York: Appleton-Century, 1965.

Remak, Joachim. *Sarajevo: The Story of a Political Murder.* London: Weidenfeld and Nicolson, 1959.

Rootham, Helen, tr. *Kossovo, Heroic Songs of the Serbs.* Oxford: B. H. Blackwell, 1920.

Sebright, Georgina, and A. P. Irby. *Travels in the Slavonic Provinces of Turkey in Europe.* London: A. Strahan, 1866.

Seton-Watson, R. W. *Sarajevo: A Study in the Origins of the Great War.* London: Hutchinson, 1926.

————. *The Southern Slav Question and the Habsburg Monarchy.* London: Constable, 1911.

Stewart, Cecil. *Serbian Legacy.* London: Allen and Unwin, 1959.

Story of the Great War. Vol. 1. New York: Collier, 1916.

Temperley, H. W. V. *A History of Serbia.* London: G. Bell, 1917.

Tuchman, Barbara. *The Proud Tower: A Portrait of the World Before the War, 1890–1914.* New York: Macmillan, 1966.

ALSO, THE FOLLOWING PAMPHLETS:

Cultural History of Croatia. Zagreb, Yugoslavia: Office of Information, 1962.

Kossovo Day. London: Polsue, 1916.

Mlada Bosna. Sarajevo: Museum of the City of Sarajevo.

171

The Lay of Kossovo. The Kossovo Day Committee of Great Britain, 1917.

The Spirit of Kosovo. London: The Serbian Orthodox Church, 1945.

ALSO, THE FOLLOWING ARTICLES:

May, Arthur J. "The Archduke Francis Ferdinand in the United States," *Illinois State Historical Society Journal* (Springfield, Ill.), Sept., 1946.

Popović, Cvetko. "Contribution to the History of the Sarajevo Assassination," *Politika* (Belgrade, Yugoslavia), March 31, April 1, 3, 4, 5, 1928.

Sellers, Edith. "The Archduke Franz Ferdinand's Diary," *Fortnightly Review* (London), Nov., 1913.

————. "The Murdered Archduke," *Nineteenth Century and After* (London), Aug., 1914.

Seton-Watson, R. W. "The Archduke Francis Ferdinand," *Contemporary Review* (London), Aug., 1914.

————. "The Murder at Sarajevo," *Foreign Affairs* (New York), April, 1925.

Steed, Henry Wickham. "The Pact of Konopisht," *Nineteenth Century and After* (London), Feb., 1916.

"The Sarajevo Murder Trial," *Slavonic Review* (London), March, 1926.

Von Sosnosky, Theodor. "New Light on Franz Ferdinand," *Contemporary Review* (London), July, 1930.

West, Richard. "Martyr Princip," *New Statesman and Nation* (London), June 26, 1954.

INDEX

Albania, 64, 153-154
Alexandar, prince of Serbia, 113, 121, 153, 155-156
Allies, member nations World War I, 126
Apis, Colonel (Dragutin Dimitrijević)
  aids assassins, 74-75, 85, 86
  after assassination, 113, 155-156, 158-159, 167-168
Appel Quay, 15, 16, 17-18, 48, 88, 92, 93, 95, 100, 103, 104, 161
Austria-Hungary, before June 28, 1914, 29-31, 32, 34, 41, 45-46, 52, 56-60, 62, 63-67, 74, 89
  June 28, 1914, through World War I, 112-118, 119-123, 124-126, 127, 135, 136-137, 139, 141-146, 148-150, 155-158
  after World War I, 152-153, 160, 165, 167

Balkan League, 61-62
Balkan peninsula, 19, 25-26, 28, 29, 30, 47, 57, 60, 115, 124
Balkan Wars, First, 61-62, 63, 65, 69, 72, 113
  Second, 62, 65, 113
Belgrade, 69-70, 71, 72, 73, 75, 79, 82, 85, 105, 119-121, 128, 144, 146, 152, 153, 166
Berchtold, Count Leopold von, 116, 117, 123
Berlin, Congress of, 30-31, 44, 45
Black Hand (Union of Death), 53, 73-75, 79, 80-82, 85, 86, 114, 129, 155
Bosnia, 21, 22

Turkish occupation of, 23, 26, 28-29, 30
annexation crisis, 30-31, 46, 122, 145
Austrian occupation of, 15, 31, 44-47, 48-49, 51, 52, 58, 63, 65-69, 74, 77, 79, 81-82, 85, 89, 90, 94, 112, 113-114, 120, 129, 135, 142, 144, 145-146, 149
Rebellion of 1875, 28-29
Yugoslavia, 157, 160, 162, 167
Bulgaria, 29, 61, 62-63, 64, 69, 115, 153, 155

Čabrinović, Nedeljko, plans for assassination, 70-71, 73, 79-80, 81-82, 88, 89
  June 28, 1914, 18, 92-94, 98-99, 100, 105
  aftermath, 112, 127-130, 131-132, 138, 140, 142-143, 145, 146, 149-150, 163, 165, 167
Central Powers, member nations, 126
Chotek, Countess Sophie, courted, 38-40
  wife of Franz Ferdinand, 69, 90-91
  June 28, 1914, 92, 93, 95-101, 103-106
  after death, 107-111, 128, 132, 141
Ciganović, Milan, 73, 75, 120
Cistler, Dr. Rudolf, 145-146
Conrad, General Franz, 64, 66, 112, 115, 123
Croatia, 24, 26, 52, 54, 58, 65, 157
Čubrilović, Vaso, plans for assassination, 76-78, 81, 84, 85, 86-87
  June 28, 1914, 18, 93-94, 96, 97